TO
Beth

Keep
on
walking

D1250451

ıg to **Walk Like a Man**
Chris Wiehl Playbook

Christopher Wiehl
with John Turner

ORF PUBLISHING

Published by Waldorf Publishing
2140 Hall Johnson Road
#102-345
Grapevine, Texas 76051
www.WaldorfPublishing.com

Trying to Walk Like a Man

ISBN: 978-1-68419-837-5
Library of Congress Control Number: 2016957053

Dedication

For my mother and father, Inga and Richard Wiehl,
without whose support none of this would be possible.

Table of Contents

Foreword by Lis Wiehl

Lis Wiehl is a best-selling author and a legal analyst for Fox News. She is currently an adjunct professor of law at New York Law School, and was formerly an associate professor at University of Washington Law School.

From the time he was born, my little brother, Chris, was destined to never come in second place. His tenacity and drive powered him to New York City and then to Hollywood, from our small town upbringing in Yakima, Washington.

You could say he was destined to be an actor. And, unlike the 99% who try, he made it. His name has graced both the big and little screens for more than twenty years. That is until a brain tumor dealt a devastating blow.

Seeing my kid brother's head bandaged in the hospital, after his operation, is an image that still haunts me today. But, like a real fighter, Chris survived and battled back. He continued auditioning and securing roles, all the while learning to hear out of only one ear. He's branched out to writing and producing movies, The Devil Dolls being his latest. My little brother Chris is not only Trying to Walk like a Man, he *does* walk like a man—a true man.

He has taken on the most imaginable pain and suffering. Gotten up. Dealt with it every day. And moved on to help others. He is my hero. This book will help you and me in ways I'm still beginning to imagine. Let's take the journey together...

Introduction

Welcome. I'm Chris Wiehl, an actor and filmmaker. Glad you could join me. (And yeah, it's "Wiehl" like the wagon.) Let me say right here at the beginning that this book you've chosen to read—and I'm glad you're reading—will *not* be one of those smarmy, pretentious "I'm sort of well-known, so you should read and love my book because of that" kind of self-absorbed memoirs. To again use an already-overused cliché: life is a journey. And mine, like everybody's, has been fun, scary, rewarding, and heartbreaking, among many other things. I've learned lessons, been close to death (seriously—we'll get to that in a minute), laughed, loved, lost, gained…and through it all, I've tried to live as best I could. I've tried to walk like a man, as this book's title suggests. The inspiration for the title is from a song, but probably not the tune that immediately comes to mind. "Walk Like a Man" was a 1963 hit by Frankie Valli and the Four Seasons, but it's also one of Springsteen's deep cuts from his *Tunnel of Love* album, and one of my all-time favorite songs. In it, Bruce sings: "Well now, the years have gone, and I've grown, from that seed you've

sown / But I didn't think there'd be so many steps I'd
have to learn on my own…" That's what I'll do my best
to lay out here: the steps I've taken, for better or worse,
to move forward in this world. The journey is still
underway. I'm still walking. And by writing this book,
I'll try to discover things about myself—and hopefully,
you can do the same. Together we'll examine our own
lives, and figure out how to step through life the best
way we know how. Deal?

Okay. Just for form's sake, I'll give you a quick bio
so you can know who you're talking to. I was born in
1970 in Yakima, Washington, a town a couple of hours
southeast of Seattle. I grew up playing a lot of sports but
discovered my love for acting my freshman year at
Yakima Valley Community College, a school right in my
hometown. I graduated from the University of
Washington in 1993 with a degree in Drama, then within
months I won a national talent search competition held
by ABC Daytime. I moved to New York City and got an
agent and a manager, lived there for eight months, and
hated it. Moved here to L.A., said I'd give myself a year
to see what happened, and luckily within a few months, I
started booking acting gigs. I got a couple of national

commercial campaigns, then some guest star roles, then some series regulars…and twenty-three years later, here I am.

On a personal note, I started dating a woman named Sarah in 2001, and we married in 2007. Not long after that, two major events happened. First, Sarah gave birth to our son, Christian, in November of '08. And right around that time, I noticed a weird ringing in my right ear; long story short, late that December my MRI results showed I had a brain tumor adjacent to the auditory nerve of that ear. The next October I had full-fledged brain surgery, but I had some post-surgical complications. I was in intensive care for eight days, and things looked pretty grim for a couple of weeks, but I made it through. The doctors were able to successfully remove the tumor, but I'm now completely deaf in my right ear, and I'll always have a bit of a balance problem.

The best thing about having a brain tumor is that it didn't kill me. I mean, shoot, even being anywhere in the same ballpark as death can give a guy a huge amount of new perspective. I kept moving forward—of course, much more carefully, haha—and six months after my surgery I'd recovered enough to be back to work (I started shooting a *Hallmark* Christmas movie six months to the *day* after my surgery date). Unfortunately, Sarah and I separated in 2011, and now I'm just trying to be a good father to Christian. A couple years ago, I met a woman named Sharon, who has two kids herself; after dating for a while, Sharon and I bought a house in the Pacific Palisades this January and moved in together, and we're getting married in about two weeks.

So that's a park-bench bio for you. I'm not sure exactly where my journey will head next, but I know I'll keep walking. I'll keep moving forward as best I can. I'm hoping my son will read this someday, and I want to express myself here with that in mind. (And Christian: whenever and wherever you're reading this, I hope I'm doing okay thus far.) That same notion of uncertainty goes for this book. I'm not exactly sure where we'll end up, or what discoveries we'll make along the way, but I'm looking forward to putting it all on the record. I *do* know that we'll talk about what it's like to try to keep moving forward (and stay sane!) in the vicious, cutthroat entertainment industry. Right now, I'm putting the finishing touches on a horror movie called *Worry Dolls* that I wrote, produced, and starred in; it's a project I've been working on for years, and it's been the main focus of my professional life for a while now, so you're going to get plenty of earfuls about it as we go along. We'll also discuss how I've dealt with some heartbreaking marital strife; how I can continue to set a good example for Christian; and how he, I, and now Sharon and her kids, can walk on this planet together.

Because if you think about it, that's what it all comes down to. Trying to move forward the best way you know how. If you break down the actual, physical act of walking, it's one step at a time. You use your leg muscles to raise your foot, then different muscles to straighten your leg and extend it forward, then you relax the muscles and plant that foot; then you repeat the process with the other leg. And all the while, your brain monitors what's going on, making sure you stay balanced while each leg repeats the raise-extend-plant process. And whether you walk slowly or briskly, you're making progress. You're *moving forward*. And eventually, you'll arrive at where you're going.

And that's life, isn't it? A series of steps, whether big or small, to propel us forward in the world. And if we're living, we're still walking. And I'm glad you're taking this particular walk with me.

Ready? Let's go.

Chapter 1:
Hiking, GPA's and Broken Legs

That Friday night, I thought that if I fell back asleep, I might never wake up again.

I was in the Intensive Care Unit at St. Vincent Medical Center, a hospital in the Koreatown district of L.A. It was three days post-brain surgery, and because of my morphine drip I was drifting in and out of consciousness. (My memory recalls it in screenplay format: FADE IN…FADE TO BLACK…FADE IN…FADE TO BLACK…) Earlier that evening, I'd been moved from the Neuro Recovery Unit upstairs, where I was recuperating from surgery to remove the brain tumor, to the general ICU on a lower floor. They'd moved me because my brain was leaking fluid, and for a critical situation like that, I would be better off in the general ICU than the Neuro one (which had reduced staff on weekends, and didn't receive patients on Fridays in the first place).

The problem was, the general ICU nurses lacked the knowledge to handle my specific issue. I (sort of) recall someone from Neuro Recovery explaining to an ICU nurse how to monitor the drainage of the fluid, but I remember that the nurse was Asian, and thus didn't speak English very well…it seemed to me that she didn't really understand the details of how to do it.

And to make matters worse, through the morphine haze I noticed the Asian nurse trying to explain how to handle the procedure to another nurse, and this one was Hispanic. So, I'm fading in and out, fluid from my damn *brain* is leaking out my nose, and we had three different languages being tossed around trying to figure out how to keep me alive.

At some point, I remember, I noticed a small wooden cross on the wall across the room. And for some unexplained reason, that cross had an enormous, empowering effect on me. Though I've never been particularly religious, I *am* very spiritual, and at that moment I prayed to God to help me make it through…to help me get home and start my life with my newborn son.

My prayer worked. I demanded that the nurses bring me a phone, and I called my wife, who'd just gotten home from visiting me all day. I told her to by all means come back, and when I explained the reason why, she and my parents jumped back in the car and rushed to the hospital again. Meanwhile, I appealed to the nurses to find my doctor and have him further explain how to handle the drainage issue. They did so, and once he gave them step-by-step instructions on how to do it, they were fine. The crisis itself faded to nothing.

But that moment I saw that cross on the wall was a defining one. I knew that, somehow, I had to find a way to keep moving forward—to be proactive in handling the situation.

And I will always think of that moment as the beginning of my New Normal.

I made it through. A couple of weeks later I went home. The doctors told me I wouldn't be able to work for at least a year, but I was blessed to be able to go back to work six months later. I was completely deaf in my right ear, I had trouble walking straight, and I'd get tired at the drop of a hat, but I was able to do it.

It was my New Normal. I had to relearn things— how to hear sounds on my right side, for example, or how to keep the world from spinning when I stood up too fast—that had previously been automatic. I had to concentrate on performing simple tasks that I used to do with no thought at all; though these things have gotten easier, I'm still relearning how to better do them, and I may always be doing so.

The problem was, my New Normal kept changing. And the biggest adjustment of all was that as time went by, Sarah and I slowly came to the realization that we'd be better off not married to each other. We were just too different. So, as I would get used to one idea of my new reality, the bar would move, if that makes sense. I'll paraphrase Springsteen again: I was finding it hard to take one step forward without taking two steps back.

When I got home from the hospital, I spent a lot of time with my newborn son. I would sit and hold him in my arms and marvel at his…his *newness*, I guess. His life had just begun, and it was untarnished by the world; he had yet to face any life-changing situations like the ones in which I was currently embroiled. He was a blank slate, waiting to be shaped by everything he experienced. *Tabula rasa*, the psychologists call this undefined state.

Tabula rasa…

* * * *

I was born on a Thursday morning.

I'm not sure that's earth-shatteringly important, but it's something my mom has always proclaimed with enthusiasm, so I figured I'd share. The time and date of that Thursday morning was 5:36 a.m. on October 29, 1970, and the place was Yakima, Washington. Yakima is a large agricultural town—lots of apples, grapes, pears, wine, and cherries, etcetera—that's a little over a hundred miles southeast of Seattle, and directly adjacent to Mount Rainier National Park and the Cascade Mountains. My dad was an attorney and a former FBI agent, and Mom was an English professor at Yakima Valley Community College right there in town. (Also of note is that she was a Danish immigrant—more on that later too.) When I was born, my parents already had a daughter, Lis, who was nine. And if the name Lis Wiehl sounds familiar, it's because she's a well-known legal analyst who appears weekly on Fox News, and she's published over a dozen books.

A bit of back-story on my family: my parents met at the University of Washington (which I'll subsequently refer to a lot, and thus will call "U-Dub" from here on out, since that's its nickname to everybody back home).

My dad was in law school, and my mom was a foreign exchange student from Denmark getting her Ph.D. in English. They met, got married, then Dad joined the FBI. They had Lis, then moved to Utah for a bit, then they went to Dallas because Dad was one of the agents assigned to the Kennedy assassination. (While living in Dallas, he also traveled to Mississippi a few times to deal with some of the racial tension that was going on there.) Several years after that, they moved back to Yakima— Dad's hometown—and he left the FBI and became an attorney. So by the time I was born, Dad had a good job at a law firm, and Mom was teaching at YVCC. According to them, Lis had been bugging them for a baby brother, and on that Thursday morning she got her wish.

And shoot: when it comes down to it, I had a wonderful childhood. Mom and Dad were strict but fair; they also both worked full-time, so I was pretty much a latchkey kid from a young age. All in all, our folks taught Lis and me to be very self-reliant; I was into athletics, and I often found myself having to get rides to and from games from other kids' parents. My own folks, because they both worked, couldn't come to many of my soccer or baseball games, and it was always a treat when they were able to make it to one.

I mentioned them being strict. They didn't rule with an iron fist or anything, but there were some things that were required from Lis and me—the most absolute of which was grades. As long as we made a 3.0, we could do pretty much everything we wanted. But if we didn't…well, hell had no fury, I'll just say that. And I will also say this: I was an outright *master* at getting a three-point-oh-oh-oh-oh-oh-oh…oh. Mom and Dad would kid me about it, but hey: at least I was consistent.

The only time I didn't make a 3.0, I learned a tough lesson. It was the winter quarter of fourth grade, I believe, and I brought my report card home. I had a 2.8. So they promptly yanked me from baseball that coming spring, which to me as a nine-year-old was utterly devastating. But I never made below a 3.0 (oh-oh-oh…) again. And it instilled in me a practice that has since been indispensable: *doing what's necessary.* To use the same vent as what we've been talking about already: if you do what needs to be done, it betters the chances for progress. Know what I mean? It keeps you from *re*-gressing. It roots you in place. Then the progress itself—

and we'll get to all this eventually—is in part determined by your priorities. By discovering precisely what needs doing in the first place. And *that's* what starts the momentum and determines the directions you'll take once you're moving forward.

Okay, digression over. Anyway: something else that was big in our house was frugality. My folks did okay moneywise, and I never really wanted for anything as a kid, but I learned the fundamental concept of working for what you wanted. I remember that my first allowance as a kid was fifty cents a week; though I'm sure my folks could've afforded giving me more, they started small and increased the weekly amount as I got older.

A lot of summers back then, my family would take trips to Europe, and our journey usually included a stop in Denmark to visit Mom's side of the family. That said, I remember being in the grocery store once—I must've been eight or nine—and Mom had a ton of coupons to give to the cashier. (Up till then, I'd never understood exactly why she clipped so many coupons. She and Dad had pretty good jobs, I thought, so what difference would saving ten cents on a box of Wheaties make?) I remember feeling embarrassed, and being like, "Jeez,

Mom, all these coupons, with these people waiting in line behind us?"

When we got in the car, she set me straight. "All those people in line? More than likely, they're not saving for a trip to Europe this summer," she said. "These coupons help us go." And that was an epiphany for me. Sure, it was an ordinary idea, that of saving up for what you wanted…but it had quite a profound effect on me.

We weren't big churchgoers. Mom was Lutheran (as most Danes are), and Dad was Presbyterian, but we didn't attend services much. Instead, we would go hiking. My folks loved being out in the wilderness of the Cascades—"Now *this* is God's church," Mom liked to say—so they would drag me out there with them most Sundays. And we would go on hikes. And not easy, "let's-walk-up-a-hill-and-be-done-with-it" hikes, either. I usually didn't want to go, but they made me. And most of the mountains we hiked up had switchbacks—steep paths that would repeatedly make 180-degree turns as you went up—that went on for half a mile or more. (The biggest one I remember was going up to Camp Muir, the base camp on Mount Rainier. It was about five miles one way, with the last two miles in snow; the base camp is as far as you can go without climbing equipment, and you reach about 10,000 feet once you get there.)

I remember that on that hike, as on most, Mom and Dad would bribe me with cookies. Like, "Christopher, once we get up to the top of these switchbacks, you can have a chocolate chip cookie." And as I was eating the cookie, we'd look back at how far we'd covered. Then, when we got to Camp Muir, Mom spread a blanket out on the snow and served us lunch. And as we sat and ate our sandwiches, we looked out at the gorgeous view of some breathtaking snow-covered mountain peaks. God's church, indeed.

I always had the same feeling when we'd reach the summit of whatever mountain we were hiking: "Okay. This was really hard. But I did it." And though I didn't know it at the time, I was gaining wisdom from those hikes. The wisdom was this: If you have a large obstacle in your path, don't be overwhelmed; instead, divide the difficulties into small segments that you can overcome more easily. And once you've gotten past all the individual small ones, you've overcome the whole thing. Then…it's on to the next.

(Sidelight: "On to the next" is my longtime agent Dan Baron's—and now my own—mantra. When I audition for a role and don't get the part, or when a show I've worked on doesn't get renewed by a network, he always says, "Oh well. On to the next." As is the nature of Hollywood, I've had to force myself to think that way too, because therapy is too expensive. And actually, hiking is something that I did a lot of when I first got to Hollywood, and it had immense therapeutic value...because of the screaming. More on all that later, when we talk about my move to L.A.)

Where were we...? Oh yeah, growing up. My folks were no-nonsense about some things, totally lax about others. It was a great mix, looking back. In my house, there was always classic literature and classical music, yet Mom wouldn't blink an eye at her ten-year-old watching an R-rated film (as long as it was good). Lis and I were taught manners and proper diction, and we had sit-down dinners at the table, often by candlelight. Though at the time I didn't always like doing the family dinner thing, it just became second nature; we'd talk about our day and such, and now, looking back, I have really fond memories of those dinners. I didn't realize this until I became an adult, but my family did a lot of bonding at that table. And it's something Sharon and I do with our kids as often as possible.

In some ways, I sort of grew up as an only child. My memories of Lis living with us are pretty scattered; since she was nine years older, and she was a foreign exchange student her senior year of high school (meaning she left home at about seventeen), I was the only kid in the house from the age of eight. So what did I do to find camaraderie? I played sports, man.

For as far back as I can remember, even as early as the first grade, I loved playing football, baseball, tennis, basketball—I loved it all. I embraced the competitiveness of it, the brotherhood, and just…the *doingness* of it, if that makes sense. As I said, my folks couldn't come to many games, but that was okay because I made a ton of friends in the process. And though Mom and Dad weren't actively involved in my playing team sports, they strongly encouraged me; my dad also inspired me to take up running, and he competed in several 10K races along with me, starting when I was about nine. I learned some great life lessons from those races: pacing myself, building character, and finishing strong.

By the time I was twelve, I was playing tournament tennis. And unfortunately, I'd started developing a bit of a temper. You can see where this is going: I was starting to act like a prepubescent John McEnroe, honestly. And once again, Mom set me straight.

She was watching a match of mine, and in disgust, I threw my racket after a bad shot. And...I think Mom was pretty keyed into my temperament because Dad had had a pretty fiery temper earlier in their marriage. (Luckily, he'd learned to control it better by the time I was around.) But after the match, she marched up and told me what was what. "Listen: that is unacceptable. No woman is ever gonna love you if you have a strong temper like that. So you need to put yourself in check, mister."

Though at the time I didn't really understand the implications of her admonishment, that little scene was burnished into my brain. And even now, all these years later, when I feel myself getting ready to lash out in anger, what do I do? I put myself in check, mister.

Now, about my sister Lis: for the most part, she was a great older sister. She always took good care of me, and she was very nurturing. Like I said, she left home when I was still pretty young, so I don't have a lot of memories of her being there. But I do remember going to some of her track meets—she was a distance runner—and I remember her being extremely determined. (That's a trait I know she's always had, and one she's utilized to an incredible extent in her legal and broadcasting careers.) I think that overall, Lis was more the "big-city" type than me, and knew she'd be more suited for a place like NYC (where she lives now). Shoot, until I decided to become an actor, I'd figured I'd spend my life in Yakima; though L.A. is my home now, I only moved here out of necessity. (Again, more on that later.)

As I've mentioned, Mom was Danish, so…she wasn't your typical American housewife. Lis and I were exposed to the arts a pretty good bit as kids. There was always classical music playing in the house, and a lot of great books lying around. And I distinctly remember the first play I ever saw, too. It was at the community college, I was about eleven, and it was theatre-in-the-round (the audience on all four sides of the stage, in other words). I thought it was just incredible how these actors would walk in and put on the show surrounded by all those people. I was just enraptured by the whole experience, but I wouldn't get bitten by the acting bug for a few years yet.

Even so, I was already learning to express myself. Since Dad was an attorney, and Mom was an English professor, we were naturally expected to express (and *explain*) our points of view about things. I remember having many lively debates around the dinner table, on a variety of subjects; those discussions were great templates for learning to communicate—templates I put to great use once I started acting.

So all the stuff we've just talked about may give you a pretty good idea about my formative years. Simply put, I did a lot of performing—but it was on athletic fields instead of stages. Honestly, I didn't know anything about acting as a youngster, and didn't actually *do* any performing until that first year at YVCC. No, when I was a kid, I carried around a bookbag like all the others, only mine was filled with various balls. If there was a sport that required a ball to play it, I had that ball in my bag. And I remember one time one of my folks wondered aloud if I ever carried any books in there. Which I did. On occasion.

As I got older, I continued playing sports, and starting in middle school I went to a larger school across town. For one thing, because it was in a higher classification there was a lot more competition—in both the school's own teams and in the games against other schools. I played football, among other sports…until the eighth grade, when one day during practice I shattered my leg from a vicious hit by another kid. We were doing a tackling drill, and I was running with the ball when the kid came in low to tackle me; I planted my left leg to turn, and he just plowed right through it. The hit destroyed my tibia and fibula, and it must've looked like what happened to Joe Theismann on national TV back in the 80s, when his lower leg broke and bent into a ninety-degree angle. In any case, it was disgusting. One kid threw up, and another kid quit the team right then and there. And Mom, who'd not liked football in the first place, told me my gridiron days were over, mister.

Needless to say, I didn't play sports of *any* kind for a few months. I was brokenhearted. I loved football, and I was a pretty fast receiver, but I will say that my brief experience with the game was a tremendous boon to a role I played some twenty-odd years later, a role that's been one of the biggest and most challenging of my career. (What role was it, you ask? Haha. Keep reading, buddy.)

I did, however, keep playing baseball and running track once my leg healed. And since they were both spring sports, I had to pick one. I chose track. And I'm glad I did, because not only was I pretty good at it, but I also learned several invaluable life lessons—in persistence and focus, among other things.

Our high school track coach was a guy named Phil English, and he was awesome. He worked our still-developing asses off, and he taught me the importance of preparation. That if you wanted to be faster than the guy in the next lane, you had to practice more than him. I learned a lot of my discipline for acting from track—that to have a chance to win (or get a particular part, as the case may be), you have to be as well-prepared as possible. And the best way to do that is to go over it…and over it…and over it. Then repeat.

I competed in the 100, 200, and 400-meter races. The strategy for the 100 and the 200 were basically the same: start strong, and give it all you have for the duration. The 400, meanwhile, was a different race entirely. Your start isn't as critical, but you have to get a good stride going…but then at about 300 meters, you feel like a bear jumps on your back. And the secret to that race, Coach English taught me, was how you finish. How you deal with that bear those last hundred meters. And I learned that the best way to finish that race (and *any* difficult task, really) is to dig deep. You have to just figure out how to give a little extra. You have to learn to carry the bear, to embrace the pain. And the more you do that, the more comfortable you are doing it.

Socially, I did okay. I wasn't super-popular, but I wasn't really unpopular, either; I had my circle of friends, and we hung out on weekends, had parties, etcetera—typical adolescent nonsense that seemed momentous at the time, but in retrospect meant very little. One memory that stands out is something that happened my junior year: I was talking with a girl in my class about what we thought our adult lives would be like. And I remember saying how I thought I would do something really important, that a lot of people would notice. She said she thought she'd end up doing something important as well. So we made a pact to discuss it again at our ten-year high school reunion (which we did, and I think you'll find great meaning in that conversation when we get to it.)

My folks continued "raising me right": Mom got me into reading more classical literature, and Dad, not through grandiose illustrations but from just living a clean, uncomplicated life, taught me the meaning of character. And by the time I graduated high school, I was ready to step into the world as a man.

College was next, obviously. But before we talk about that, let's review: born on a Thursday, sports, hiking up Mount Rainier, put yourself in check mister, kid threw up when I broke my leg, ran track, graduated.

Are we good? Okay. On to the next.

Chapter 2:
Destiny Defined

(July 22)

One word.

They want to change one single word, but that tiny modification might make an enormous difference.

For the past six years, I've poured my heart and soul into making a horror movie called *Worry Dolls,* a film about some tiny dolls that inadvertently cause murder and mayhem. My screenwriting partner, Danny Kolker, and I spent a good two years perfecting the script. It took us another year and a half, I guess, to raise the money to make it (about a million bucks in all). We spent a couple months in Mississippi in 2014 shooting the film, then at least another year doing editing, sound design, color correction, and composing the score. Once all that was finished and we basically had a completed product, we looked for a distributor, which these days is really hard to find for small-budget films like ours. Long story short, after months of looking we finally closed a deal for domestic distribution with IFC. At this point, we're putting the final touches on the film for IFC to do a domestic release at theaters here in L.A. and in New York City, while simultaneously releasing it on various video-on-demand services, on September 16th.

This morning I got a call from an IFC rep, who said that they were, well, worried about *Worry Dolls* as a title. It doesn't have instant recognition as a horror movie title, the guy said, and some might dismiss it as being silly. "We like *The Devil's Dolls* better," he said. "How does that sound?" For one thing, he went on, most VOD services list their titles alphabetically; when people are browsing their Netflix or Amazon Prime for something to watch, they're a lot more likely to pick something in the D's (like *The Devil's Dolls*) than one buried way down in the W's (which is where *Worry Dolls* would end up).

I hate it. I think we have a great title in *Worry Dolls*, as it really captures more of the essence of the story. Even so…it'll be a sacrifice I'll have to make. We'll have to redo the posters and all the promotional artwork, but fighting a major company like IFC over something as relatively minor as a simple title change is a battle I'll ultimately lose. And those kinds of artistic compromises happen on an all-too-regular basis.

In situations like this, I've had to learn to put myself in check, mister. Or more specifically, I have to leave my ego out of it. And the weird thing is, in the acting business, my ego is something I often try to use to my advantage. Not out of vanity or conceit, mind you, but because having a huge amount of confidence--possessing a certain "swagger," if you will—can often be the difference in booking or not booking a gig.

My ego. Everybody has one—some big, some small. (As you'd expect, I tend to put myself in the former category.) And a valuable trick amongst us actors is knowing when and how to use it. And the best way of learning how to use our personalities to our advantage is knowing ourselves. (Cliché, I know—but stay with me.)

I probably learned more about myself, about who it was I would actually become, during my freshman year in college.

* * * *

Unfortunately (or fortunately, depending on how you look at it), my three-point-oh-oh-oh high school GPA wasn't good enough to gain entrance to U-Dub, so my first year I went to YVCC, with a plan to transfer to U-Dub as a sophomore. So I enrolled, and one of my mom's friends, Ellie Haffernan, was an academic counselor and basically handpicked my classes for me. Going in, I really didn't know yet what I wanted to study, but I knew I liked being in front of people, speaking in front of them, etcetera. I honestly assumed I would end up being an attorney like my father and sister, go to law school, and practice law in Yakima like my dad. (Obviously, that isn't what happened.) I had the counselor enroll me in an Intro to Drama class…and that was one of the best decisions I've ever made.

The instructor for that class was named Dr. George Meschke, who was the head of the YVCC drama program—and the man solely responsible for biting me with the acting bug. (More like an out-and-out acting *chomp,* really.) Other than the few plays I'd seen as a kid, I really had had no exposure at all to the theatre, so I was *tabula rasa* for sure when it came to acting. I loved both the class and Dr. Meschke's magnetic personality, and I was hooked from the first lecture.

Dr. Meschke talked me into auditioning for the first play of that school year, and I did so with no hesitation.

The show was a children's play called *Six Who Pass While the Lentils Boil,* and it was quite a departure from the normal YVCC drama offerings. But Kendall Hall, where stage plays were normally put on, was being renovated that second quarter, so Dr. Meschke decided to produce a minimalist children's play that we could easily perform at local elementary schools.

Somehow, I got the lead. I played David, a little boy who is presented with numerous moral dilemmas while his mother makes soup. We took the show to six or seven schools, if memory serves, and performed it for first- and second-graders. And let me tell you: I don't think I could've asked for a better experience in my first acting role. Because kids that age—about the same age as Christian is now—are totally honest, for better or worse. Which means that unlike most adults, who will feign interest simply out of manners, if kids don't like something, they'll just ignore it. So not only did I have to do the work of building the character, I had to toil extra hard to keep their interest. It was trial by eight-year-old fire, no doubt.

But stepping out on the stage gave me thrills unlike any I'd ever experienced. Just to have every single person in the room be totally focused on what you say, how you move, how you *act*, was…it electrified me. Even in the first performance, it felt completely natural. And after the last show one of the other cast members, a guy named Lee Gilliam who was a little older and had more experience than I did, said, "Hey, Chris, nice job. Ever thought about doing more of this?" And that was it. I was hooked.

Unbeknownst to me at the time, I was about to do more of it. A *helluva* lot more.

A few weeks later, I found out that the next show at YVCC would be *The Elephant Man.* It was a heavyweight drama about the life of John Merrick, the horribly deformed British man who became a national spectacle in the late 1800s. I bet you're familiar with the 1980 film starring Anthony Hopkins and John Hurt, but maybe not with the stage play. The main difference between the two is that the film uses heavy prosthetics to make John Hurt closely resemble the real-life Merrick, while the play has the actor simply contort his body and speech to suggest the deformities. The role of John Merrick was a complex, challenging one for any actor…and I and my competitive self wanted it badly.

Because I was an acting rookie, I didn't really know much about preparing for an audition. So I studied the script some, worked up my best Standard British and Cockney accents—the character uses both—and gave the best audition I could. Listening to the other actors reading for the role, I figured there was no *way* Dr. Meschke would cast me as Merrick.

I figured incorrectly. I got it. And I was pumped. We jumped into rehearsal right away, and Dr. Meschke had us for six nights a week. The characters of Merrick and Dr. Treves pretty much carry that play, so Friday and Saturday rehearsals were with just the two of us. And during that month of rehearsing, and then for the nine performances, I learned more about the nuts and bolts of acting than at any time since. I was in great shape, so I was able to handle the physical aspects of the role. And I was able, with Dr. Meschke's guidance, to really empathize with the unbelievable struggles John Merrick must've endured. I would look at photos of him in real life and try to imagine how he must have felt when other people saw him. It broke my heart. I tried my best to let that vulnerability be a part of the character, and it worked pretty well.

Looking back, there's no doubt in my mind: playing John Merrick was a destiny-defining moment for me. I got several standing ovations—the first standing O's at Kendall Hall in many years, I was later told—and I won some statewide awards, including Best Male Actor at a Small College. My buddy Lee Gilliam, who wasn't in the show but saw it, said to me afterward, "You got it, kid. Don't ever stop." And my dad, whom I knew hadn't been sure about me going into acting in the first place, was almost as thrilled as I was, I think. "Okay," he told me backstage after he saw the show opening night. "You have to do this." And that was the best vote of confidence I could've gotten.

Performing, for me, was…I don't know. Natural? Easy? No, not that. It was *innate.* That's it. Right from the beginning. I realized even then that I had a talent for make-believe. And what I mean by that is that I found I had the ability to use my body, my mind, and most importantly, my *heart* to become someone else for a while. It was more than just "pretending." It was more than just "acting" like someone else. It was *being* that other person. It was walking as them, talking as them, and feeling all of life's emotions *as* them. That's the best way I know to describe it. And in the twenty-five-odd years since I first started acting, I've learned a multitude of ways to refine that…but during my time working on *The Elephant Man*, I discovered one huge, basic concept: that *acting is being.*

Dr. Meschke saw that in me, God rest his soul. (Tragically, he died several years ago when he choked on some food while eating at a restaurant. That was an unbelievably sad day. He was such a good man, and an absolutely extraordinary director. I know that I, and many others, I'm sure, feel his loss even now…but I believe that his legacy will continue, in the characters created by all the actors he so brilliantly taught.) And I think, looking back, that Dr. Meschke further instilled in me some of the same values that Coach English had in high school track—namely, that to do your best, you have to *put in the work.* You have to be prepared. They both saw that I had some talent, and some passion and hunger to go along with it. Coach English would say, "Yes, you're fast, but you have to work hard to be faster." And Dr. Meschke, likewise, would say, "Yes, you're a good actor, but you have to work to be better." He taught me that when you prepare for a role, the first (and smartest) thing to do was to read the script fifty times. You have to go over it…and over it…and over it (sound familiar?) until the words become your own. And *then* you're ready to start building the character.

Dr. Meschke also helped me learn to trust my own instincts—and in a larger sense, to trust myself. He gave me a great foundation by allowing me to make a lot of my own acting choices. And I will say that he put a lot of faith in me when he cast me as John Merrick. Shoot, it was only the second play I'd ever done! I think there were several other actors, all of whom were more experienced, who were equally capable of handling that role, and for him to give it to me was a bit of a risk. Some of the other actors seemed to be a little suspect of me at first because I was so green, but they were very professional about it when all was said and done.

So, by the end of that school year, I'd established an identity for myself. I was going to be an actor. (I didn't really know how yet, or when, or where, but I *did* know I'd one day perform professionally.) And you'll be happy to hear that during that one year at YVCC, I was able to surpass my academic career three-point-oh-oh-oh GPA by a lot. (I think I had like a 3.7 or something.) So I transferred to U-Dub the next year full of vim, vigor, and confidence.

And boy, was I going to need it.

* * * *

Going to the University of Washington had always been sort of a given for me. My grandfather went there, and both my parents did too—that's where they met, remember—so I was basically a Husky even in the womb. I transferred there my sophomore year, and majored in drama; The School of Drama at U-Dub was excellent, so I knew I would get some great training...but it was all theatre. Going in, I was already sort of thinking about how to get some work in film and/or TV in NYC or Hollywood, so I was sort of surprised that none of the classes offered anything on how to act for the camera. Thinking about it now, the people running the U-Dub School of Drama were sort of purists about theatre acting. (My guess is that's the case with a lot of college drama departments.) Could be that's changed in the twenty-five-odd years since, but my memory is that I received very little training in how to be a professional actor, and absolutely *zero* training in acting for the camera.

But listen: I don't want you to think my experience at U-Dub was all bad. Overall, I received a fantastic education, and I learned a whole lot from my acting classes about building a character, among other things. I was in some great plays, like Sam Shepard's *True West* and an adaptation of a German tragedy called *Woyzeck*. But my experience was in retrospect a bit frustrating, because years later when I started getting TV gigs, I had no clue of what to do. I basically had to learn on the fly—how to hit my exact mark, and definitely how not to "overact." As you can imagine, stage and camera acting are two different mediums. Stage work is so external, and a good theatre actor can emote to the guy sitting in the back row while not looking ridiculous to the guy right up front. And when you act for the camera, a sort of universal rule of thumb is: "If you think it, the audience will see it." They're two very different acting styles, for sure. I think good actors can do both, but if you're trained in only one style, you're sort of behind the eight ball when it comes to learning the other.

As an upperclassman, I was really starting to believe I could compete in the Hollywood acting market, but the classes I was taking just weren't aligning with that. Example: I took an upper-level acting course that required students to audition for a spot in the class. I got in, and right away we started learning the Suzuki acting method, which focuses on your breathing and emphasizes ways to find a character's "animal energy." It's a brilliant, extremely popular method—for the *theatre.* I honestly thought it was for the birds, and didn't really see how that was going to help me audition for a cereal commercial or something; when I expressed my distaste for what we were doing, the instructor wasn't too pleased, and she and I sort of butted heads for the rest of the semester.

When it comes down to it, I was sort of an odd duck in the U-Dub theatre department—for the reason I just explained, yes, but also because I was in a fraternity. I pledged Sigma Chi my sophomore year, since my father had been in the same chapter, and I had a great time. Parties on Tuesdays, Thursdays, and Saturdays—the old "work hard, play hard" course of study. But I will say that none of my frat brothers were theatre majors, nor were any of the theatre guys also in a frat. Those two worlds are *completely* divergent, so I had a bit of difficulty fitting in with the theatre kids.

But again, my time at U-Dub was altogether exceptional. I also took some writing courses, and really began to understand the nuts and bolts of what makes a good story. And as a Huskies football devotee since birth, I was pumped when U-Dub went to the Rose Bowl for three years straight, and won the national championship at the end of the '91 season.

Every two or three years, I feel honored to be invited back to U-Dub to talk to the drama kids about life as a professional actor. While I don't mention my perceived lack of training at U-Dub for acting for the camera—it's not really my place to do so—I *am* brutally honest with them about the acting business. "Listen," I tell them, "if you're doing this for fame, fortune, and notoriety, then by all means, get out of it. Go do something else." If they think there is something else they can do that will make them reasonably happy, I say, they should change majors…because the chances of them making a living as an actor (or a writer, or a producer) are almost insurmountable. I talk more about the business side of it—about how to maintain a good work ethic. Because first and foremost, acting is a *business*, just like plumbing or real estate. You have to know your product, and more importantly, you have to know how to earn money from it. And if those kids didn't realize that, they were in for a whole lot of disappointment.

On June 19, 1993, I graduated from the University of Washington with a Bachelor of Arts in Dramatic Arts. At that point, I knew my product—me—pretty well, and though I wasn't entirely sure yet how I'd earn money from it, I had a burning desire to learn how. And it wouldn't be long before I got an incredible crash course…one that was more difficult than I could've imagined. Here's a five-word preview: Security guard at The Gap.

Chapter 3:
The Big Apple is Rotten

(July 30)

Today, my house became a home.

The reason for that evolution is that Sharon and I got married. We had an intimate ceremony on a bluff overlooking the Pacific Ocean, a couple of blocks from our house in the Pacific Palisades. It was a small, private affair, attended by family and a few close friends; a guy named Hayden, who is our manny (our "male nanny"), is an ordained minister, so he performed the ceremony. It was a quick, beautiful thing: Christian was the Best Man, and Sharon's daughter Trista was the Maid of Honor. We said some vows we'd written, exchanged rings, then we all had a champagne toast. After that, we walked back to our home and had an informal reception in the backyard, with about fifty folks attending. We had a temporary wooden dance floor set up in the yard, food was provided by a local taco truck, and everybody had a blast. Next week Sharon and I are flying to St. Barts, where we've rented a nice little beach house, for our honeymoon…then it's back here to L.A. to begin our lives as husband and wife.

I think for both Sharon and me, our marriage is like coming home, both literally and figuratively. We've each married our best friend, our union is a safe harbor…all the usual clichés apply. But today we're not just starting a new chapter, we're starting a whole new book. Sharon and I have both been married before, and I know we both went through a lot of pain and sorrow during those marriages. So our wedding today was a way of closing the book on that suffering, and opening a new one filled with love and support. Sharon's kids, Brett and Trista, and my son Christian…we're all part of a unit now. *One* unit. Our society is so full of sadness in family matters—high divorce rates, broken homes, lack of parental approval—that to have a home full of positivity and happiness is an unbelievable blessing. For me, for Sharon, and for the kids too. I'm incredibly excited to find out what our future has in store for us.

Speaking of being excited about the future…

* * * *

After I graduated, it wasn't long before I was on the fast-track to acting success, baby. (Or that's what I thought at the time.) Graduation was in June, and early that fall I hit the jackpot: I won a national talent search sponsored by ABC Daytime. They went to cities around the country holding auditions, and I went to the one in Seattle; long story short, I won the whole thing. Part of the prize was that they flew me to NYC, put me up in a hotel, and arranged meetings with all the casting directors of the ABC soaps that were shooting in New York at the time (*Loving, One Life to Live, All My Children,* and etcetera). So here I was, the ink still wet on my diploma, and I'm about to land a regular gig on a national TV show. I was elated.

I also met with several managers and talent agents, and everybody—the casting directors, the managers, the agents— all told me the same thing: "You *have* to move here to New York!" I told them that of course I would! I flew back home, let my parents know what my plan was, and had a heart-to-heart talk with my girlfriend, who immediately dumped me. (No surprise there.) Then within a couple of weeks, I moved into a small studio apartment on the Upper East Side of Manhattan with one of my former fraternity brothers. It was a fifth-floor walkup. Besides my roommate, I hardly knew a soul in the entire city…but that didn't really matter to me then, because I was still pumped from winning the talent search. I thought I was unstoppable.

When I think about it now, twenty-three years later, moving to New York so soon after college was one of the worst decisions I've ever made—but it was also one of the best.

It was a horrible choice because, for one, none of the ABC Daytime casting directors offered me a job. None of the soaps had an opening for a regular role, and while they all said they would keep an eye out for a part for me, none came through. And in the following nine months that I was in New York, despite going to dozens of auditions…I never got cast for anything. I got close on a couple of commercials, but when all was said and done, I didn't book a single gig.

The good thing about that? I learned that acting was a business. I learned that to sell your product— yourself—you had to work on doing so *every single day.* I met some other actors while I was there, most of whom had been there longer than I had, and I saw that they were *constantly* doing things that would help their careers—going to auditions, yes, but also taking classes, doing shows for free, and working out to stay in good physical shape. And it was incredibly humbling to realize that many of them, despite being in New York for years, hadn't really had much success either. It was quite an eye-opening revelation, and the best learning experience I could've had.

The other benefit of my time in New York is that I connected with my first agent, a woman named Holly Lebed who worked with a small talent agency there. As it turns out, she represented me for years here in L.A., and I'm still in touch with her to this day. She went to bat for me numerous times even back then, and I'll always be grateful for her love and support—especially during a time when the Big Apple was chewing me up and spitting me out.

But anyway: here's what those nine months were like. Once I saw that ABC Daytime wasn't going to come through, I started looking for a job. I'd done some bartending in college, so I decided I'd start there. Heck, good bartenders are in demand everywhere, right? Wrong. I found out that all the bartending jobs—*all* of them—were taken, often by other out-of-work actors. Next, I figured, *Unemployed thespian? Gotta wait tables.* Being a server couldn't be all that different from bartending, right? Wrong again.

A restaurant a couple of blocks from my place hired me as a waiter…and I think I lasted about two hours. For my first training shift, I shadowed another server, and right away I realized the pace was in-flippin'-*sane*. You had to be able to do twelve things at once, and the customers—and this was probably made worse by the fact that it was NYC—were incredibly rude. This was a complete shock for me. As a bartender, if a customer was rude to you, they just didn't get their drink…so I'd usually been treated with plenty of courtesy as a bartender because I was in charge of supplying folks with booze. Serving food, on the other hand, was an entirely different ballgame, and I couldn't handle it. So not long after the dinner rush started that first night, I told my trainer I had to take a quick break. I took off my apron, put it on a wait-station counter, and walked out the door, never to return.

As the weeks went by, my bank account shrank to nearly zero, while the frequency of my hunger pangs grew exponentially. And about the time I was expecting to receive an eviction notice from my landlord…*whew*. I got a job. *Two* jobs, actually. I started working in the mornings as a personal trainer at a place called Aline Fitness. It was on about 30th Street, and I lived on 74th. And I had to walk to and from there, as I was saving my subway money for getting to auditions. So yeah. Forty-plus blocks is an *awfully* nice stroll.

Then in the evenings, I went to my other job. Yeah, you already know what I'm about to say. Security guard at The Gap.

Stop laughing. It paid the bills, okay? Actually, when I think about it now, I laugh too. It was a bit silly to me, doing that job, but I was desperate. Hey, a fella had to eat, right? When I applied there—it was on 3rd Avenue, not far from my place, thank God—they took my application, then tested me on my shirt-folding skills. And well, I won't say I failed the test, but…yeah. I failed. I remember feeling pretty discombobulated as the Gap employees—all females—had a good chuckle watching me struggle to contort the Slim Fit Pocket Tees. (Anybody who knows me personally can imagine how idiotic that was. I mean, heck, I'm in my forties, and I have no clue how to even iron.)

But at some point, the manager said, "Hey, you're a pretty big guy. How bout being a security guard?" It was an extra two bucks per hour, she said, and I'd get a walkie-talkie, the whole nine. "Perfect. Sign me up," I said. So a couple of nights later, I worked my first shift. I was one of four guys on the Gap Security Detail—stop laughing—and we wore Gap clothes while we roamed the store looking for shoplifters. And I'll be the first one to tell you: I was a *horrible* security guard. For one, I never caught anybody stealing something. (And I know people stole stuff. Because one of our duties was to count the pairs of sunglasses we had on hand at closing, and we constantly came up short. I said stop laughing!) One cool thing was that we had several celebrities—Bryant Gumbel, that girl with the big red hair in the B-52s, etcetera—who were regular customers. (To my knowledge, neither Bryant Gumbel nor the B-52s chick ever stole anything. Which, as evidenced by my lack of security skills, didn't mean they didn't.) And it's okay to laugh now. I'm not actually accusing anybody of theft, I'm just being totally un-PC for the sake of the joke.

Listen: I don't want to disrespect people who work in retail (or on the security of it). Doing that kind of work takes a particular kind of skill. I'm making fun of myself here, because I possess absolutely *none* of those skills. Even so, I was somehow able to fool myself into enjoying the job...mainly because my diet choices expanded greatly from either Ramen noodles or PB&J. I was livin' *large* eating Campbell's Chunky, buddy!

And for better or worse, that pretty much sums up my NYC experience. I'd walk forty blocks to my personal trainer job in the morning, then go to an audition in the afternoon (if I had one, that is, and I often didn't), then go *not* chase any lawbreakers at The Gap in the evening. I was frustrated, lonely, and extremely broke. As you can imagine, New York is not a fun city to live in when you have no money. It's like...oh, I don't know. When you live in NYC, you have to constantly be at the very top of your game, both professionally and personally. Everything is right in your face at every waking moment. And honestly? At that age, I didn't have a clue. I hadn't even *started* taking those proverbial steps forward. I was just learning how to stand, to be honest.

And being in that city, at that time in my life, I was just grist for the mill.

By that next June, I'd pretty much had it. As a West Coast Kid, I figured L.A. would be a much better fit for me. And boy, was I right about that.

Chapter 4:
Six Months, Plus a Couple of Years

(Sept. 19)

This past Friday was the premiere of *The Devil's Dolls,* the horror movie I've spent six years making. It was to be a weekend of celebration, of long lines at the box office, of rave reviews…it would be the unofficial recognition of Christopher Wiehl, juggernaut filmmaker.

Only it wasn't that. At all. In fact, this past weekend was one of the worst in recent memory.

As is the case with many problems in the entertainment business, it all came down to money. Since the movie was independent, we had to do some creative budgeting, juggle some of the funding, yada yada. As it turns out, our juggling act didn't work very well. We shot the movie in Mississippi, and were expecting the State to issue us a rebate on some of the in-state spending we did; it was quite a sizable chunk of cash. Only the rebate was nowhere near the amount we thought we'd receive, which left us over $80,000 in the red. We'd earmarked that money to pay back some of our debtors, and when they found out they weren't getting paid as soon as they thought, they didn't take it too well. In fact, one debtor attempted to put a lien on the film, meaning he would own it outright. So I spent all day Friday (and part of the next week) on the phone with him, with various attorneys, and with my other producers. In the end, we got it worked out (mainly because one of the other producers agreed to take money out of his own retirement fund to help pay the guy off), but the whole thing just stank.

Then to make matters worse, IFC's theatrical rollout was…less than impressive, I'll say that. The theater in L.A. where the film was shown was tiny—*maybe* sixty seats—and though I wasn't at the New York premiere, it's my understanding that that was the case with the theater there too. Nor did IFC do much promotion for the premiere, neither for the theatrical release or the video-on-demand. When Sharon and I got to the L.A. theater Friday night, I nearly had a meltdown when I saw how small it was. Oh, I put on my happy face for the screening and the Q&A that followed it…but afterward we went to the nearest bar, and I proceeded to get stinking drunk. It was heartbreaking. And when all is said and done, we'll probably end up losing all the money we put into it.

It's par for the course in the entertainment industry. I worked like a dog for half a decade on this film. It's eighty-five minutes long; for every minute of that eighty-five, we probably spent five *hundred* minutes filming, editing, producing, and scoring it. I'm proud of it. In addition to being scary as hell, the film has unique, thought-provoking appeal. I think—and I've had other people tell me, and I don't think they were just blowing sunshine up my ass—that this movie would compete with a lot of mainstream, studio-backed horror films. Unfortunately, the movie business is unbelievably competitive…and ours just got lost in the shuffle.

I'll keep going. I'll move on to the next thing. (On to the next, right?) For this project, in particular, I have a responsibility to everybody else who invested in it to try and make it as successful as possible. And once the *Worry D*—shit. *DEVIL'S Dolls* situation comes to some kind of resolution, I'll look forward to my next project. Why? Because that's what it means to be a professional. Because *that's what successful people do.*

And *how* will I move on from this? Two reasons. I have love, and I have hope. I have a wife and kids who love me regardless of whether I win or lose, and who will support me in anything I do. I also have a love for creating things. And as long as I can support myself and my family through my creativity, I'll keep doing it.

And when the opportunity presents itself, I'll make another movie. And I'll *hope* that it does better than this one. Meantime, I'll keep going to auditions. Some parts I'll get, some I won't. But I hope I'll get them all.

What's that old proverb? "Fall seven times, get up eight." I'll come back from this. And if I get knocked down again, well, shoot, I'll get back up. Because that's life. That's the journey. That's how you keep walking forward.

Twenty-three years ago, my professional journey began taking shape when I traded the East Coast for the West. But it was *slooowww* going at first.

* * * *

When I left NYC, I told my manager and my agent that I was going to go back to Seattle to sort of take stock in my life and figure out what my next move would be. Summer of '94, this would've been, and I went back home a little older, wiser, and humbler. That modesty would have to continue, too: the first job I had upon my return was as a towel boy at the Seattle Athletic Club. I cleaned the bathrooms, did the laundry, and tried my best to avoid making eye contact with the club members, some of whom had been my fraternity brothers at U-Dub. Here I was, a college-educated guy, just back from failing in my attempt to be a star actor in New York, and I was washing people's dirty towels.

For a time, I had my doubts about succeeding as a professional actor. I was really reaching a low point. I took the Law School Admission Test—the good ol' LSAT—because I figured I would eventually need to enact my secondary plan of being an attorney. But it took three or four months to get the test scores back...and in retrospect, that delay changed my life.

At some point during those three or four months, I said to myself, *Dammit. You know what? I owe it to myself to give L.A. a shot.* I mean, what did I really have to lose? I figured I would go down to L.A., give it everything I had, and if it didn't work out, I'd come back and go to law school. For better or worse, I decided, I had to try. I talked to my folks about it, and they said that as long as I gave L.A. my very best, I had their blessing. I also—and this was another beautiful twist of fate—I also called Holly Lebed, my agent in New York, hoping her agency hadn't completely cast me aside. Lo and behold, when I told her I wanted to try to find work in Hollywood, she said, "Oh my gosh. We're already here! We just finished moving to L.A. ourselves!" It was perfect.

So early one morning in October of that year, I loaded up my Jeep, and with my dad following me in his Volvo, we set out down Interstate 5 to Los Angeles. I had all my worldly possessions: a microwave, a TV, a stereo, and some clothes. The two-day trip took us through the gorgeous Pacific Northwest countryside, which at that time of year was even more magnificent because of the dazzling fall colors. And that whole drive just felt—right, I guess. The scenery reinforced that feeling. I grew up a country boy, and I was really looking forward to living in a city that had some space, where either the ocean or the mountains would just be a short drive away. It was definitely preferential to the concrete world of NYC, which consisted of tall, intimidating buildings everywhere you looked.

Late that Sunday afternoon, we came around a bend in the road in the San Gabriel Mountains, and POW! There was the entire L.A. metro area spread out down in the valley ahead. (I remember feeling both excited and hopeful at that moment, as if twenty million people had been waiting for me.) A couple hours later, we arrived in Hermosa Beach, an oceanside community on the southwestern side of the city, where I lived for the first year I was here. (Luckily, a friend from college had been looking for a roommate to share her apartment there in Hermosa, so I already had a place to stay.) The day after we got there, Dad and I went to lunch, and during that meal he bestowed upon me an absolute blessing.

Our waiter was this tall, good-looking guy, and at some point, Dad said to him, "Can we ask you a question?"

"Sure," the waiter said.

"Are you from around here?"

The guy chuckled. "Actually, I'm not. I'm from Nebraska. I moved here to try to be an actor."

"Oh really," Dad responded. "How's it working out for you?"

"Honestly? Not very well." He went on to explain that he was finding it extremely difficult to have time to go to auditions because he had to work so much just to pay the bills.

Lunch went on, but a little later Dad said to me, "Seems like it'd be hard to do both. Go to work and go to auditions, I mean."

I agreed that yes, that was indeed a problem.

"Then Christopher, here's what we'll do. If you're really going to give it a go here, we'll give you enough money to live on for six months. That way you can focus your time on auditions, and you won't have to worry about bills."

I was stunned. That was the first I'd heard of that. "Dad. I —"

"Six months. If things don't go your way, after six months, you'll come home and go to law school. Agreed?"

"I...sure. Agreed. Thank you."

Looking back, I wonder how he and Mom must've felt about doing that. I mean here he was, a successful attorney, and they were letting their son cast aside a promising future of following in Dad's footsteps and becoming a lawyer himself so he could continue chasing his dream—one that had comparatively *no* promise, truth be told. I will forever be indebted to them for their support of me then, and in all the years since.

But he told me that if I was serious about making it, *truly* serious, then being an actor, even one just starting out, was a full-time job. And I had to do something to further my career *every single day*. My mind immediately flashed back to all those folks in NYC as I said that without a doubt I would do just that. (Go ahead and insert the *Rocky* theme here.)

So here I was. The world (or the Hollywood acting business, anyway) was my oyster. Luckily, since Holly and her agency had just moved here, I already had representation, which was a big plus. And right away, Holly reinforced what my Dad had said: that to get acting jobs, the first thing you had to do was *be available*. "Chris," I remember her saying at one point early on, "I don't want to hear about you going on a vacation for about the first four years. Got it?" I remember I got a cell phone—this is back when they were just becoming popular, and mine was a big, clunky flip phone about triple the size of current models—and I could only afford like ten minutes per month on it. And Holly was the only one who had the number to it, so it became like my acting Bat-phone. (Whenever it would ring I'd be like, "Heck yeah! Got an audition!") Also, that was before email became the norm, so to get scripts for auditions I'd have to drive into the city, which was about an hour one way.

I started out by going to every audition I had even a remote shot of booking, and the first month I got nothing. Neither did I the second month. Nor the third. Then, toward the end of month four, I remember, just as I was feeling the tightening in my gut when I thought about having to move back home again with my tail between my legs…I got a part. It was a national ad campaign for Lee jeans. I was pumped. And it wasn't long before I did another national spot for Coca-Cola, then I followed that with a Coors Light commercial, in which I got to appear with John Wayne.

Okay, it wasn't the living, *breathing* John Wayne, as he died in what, '79? '80? But he was spliced into it, saying lines from his movies that fit the dialogue of the commercial. I played a Marine, and in the spot—maybe you remember it? It ran during the Super Bowl that year—our drill sergeant is trying to figure out whose beer he'd found during a surprise inspection, and The Duke swaggers up and says it's his. I got to work with R. Lee Ermey, whom you probably know as the drill instructor in *Full Metal Jacket*...it was a memorable shoot, no doubt.

In the following months, I started booking gigs regularly. I did numerous commercials, mainly because I got a separate agent strictly for that (back then it was Abrams Artists; some of the Abrams agents went on to form AKA Talent Agency, which still books commercials for me now). I did a Pizza Hut spot with Pamela Anderson, then a Campbell's Soup one with Wayne Gretzky, and I was really starting to advance my career by meeting and working with people with big-time production companies. And the best thing was that I was able to call my folks and tell them that I was making some money (not much, of course, but enough to live on), and that I planned to stay in L.A. and keep after it, at least for the time being.

That first year or two, I definitely lived hand-to-mouth. Though I booked those commercials, I was still *way* out on the fringes of the Hollywood acting industry. And I knew the only way to work my way in was to put my head down and keep going. I had to keep that proverbial bear of unemployment from jumping on my back, to put it in Coach English's terms. One of the most important pieces of knowledge I gained during that period was in a class I took from Vincent Chase, who's a veteran acting coach and pretty much a Hollywood legend. (Vincent has been an acting coach in L.A. for over sixty years—some call him "the Yoda of acting"—and has coached…shoot, everybody. Marilyn Monroe, Jim Carrey, Harrison Ford, you name it. Far as I know, he's still going strong even in his late eighties.) Vincent, in all his wisdom, taught me that when all is said and done, you have to figure out a way to take the emotion out of the casting process. Yeah, you have to work hard and be prepared for every audition. But—and this took me a while to fully understand—he said the mark of a true acting professional is *learning to live with disappointment*. The difference between someone who says they want to be a professional actor, and someone who actually *does* it, is this: the novices may have some success at first, but they often hit a wall at some point early in their careers when it seems like they'll never get cast again. And unfortunately, that's what gets them. That's what makes them give up. But the pros, instead of throwing their hands up and finding another career (like being an attorney), double their efforts. They keep going, often *past* the point of what others would consider simple futility. And if you could keep going, Vincent said, if you could work on advancing your career *every single day*, eventually something would break for you. And when it did, you had to be ready.

That was music to my ears. I was already doing things daily to help my career, so I'd just keep that up. I was also fortunate that Holly and my other agents kept sending me on auditions regularly. Heck, by the time I moved into another place in Marina del Rey, I'd driven from Hermosa Beach to Hollywood so often that I could've done it with my eyes closed.

Then, at the start of my second year here, another break came. (More like a "crack," really, but a break nonetheless.) I got a small role on the first season of a new TV show called *JAG*. Even though I only had about three lines, I got a co-starring credit, which was huge. Right on the heels of that was a co-starring role on the show *Space: Above and Beyond* (and if you don't remember the show, no worries, as Fox canceled it after one season). So I was slowly working my way in— painfully slow, yes, but it was happening. Speaking of pain: I had my first instance of heartbreak during that early period, too. *No*, not from a girl, from a role I had high hopes for. Sheesh. I read for the lead in the pilot of a new sci-fi show called *The High Command*, and the director loved me. I was told I was the first choice for it. This would be the big break for me. But before they made their final decision, the director flew to New York for a few days…and on his flight back, he died of a brain aneurysm. Tragic, of course, but just as tragic (for me, anyway) was that the director that replaced him cast someone else. And I hadn't yet figured out how to live with the disappointment, so that hurt. I took it personally, and thought, *Why meeee???* Luckily, I found a way to move "on to the next" — long before it became a go-to slogan for me.

I've since discovered that every single working actor I've met has a similar story — that instance where you think you've got a great role, then…aww. And I've heard every weird reason you can think of (and some you can't) for these "casting tragedies," I'll call them. But through the years I've learned another lesson: that *there are some things you just can't control*. You may have given the best audition of your stinkin' *life*, but the casting director hated you because you look just like her ex. Or maybe the producer ate too many empanadas for lunch and had indigestion, so every time he thinks about your audition he gets a queasy feeling. Or heck, maybe the director who loved you so much dies unexpectedly. The reasons are numerous, and they're often ludicrous, but that's *just the plain reality*. It would be a few years yet before I learned that hard truth about the acting business. Something I tell beginning actors—*especially* the drama kids at U-Dub when I go back and talk to them—is: "If you're looking for 'fair,' 'just,' or 'right,' you're in the wrong business, buddy."

But I toiled on. By late '95 I moved into an apartment in Marina del Rey, another beach neighborhood somewhat closer to the city proper. 1996 was sort of a dry spot for me, in that I didn't book many acting gigs. I auditioned for some fantastic parts, too, and thought I had some of them, but nothing went my way. As I'd been taught, I kept myself busy. For one thing, I enrolled in more classes, this time at Joanne Baron/D.W. Brown Studio, one the premier acting schools in L.A.

Baron/Brown taught us the nuts and bolts of what's called the Meisner technique, a type of acting training that utilizes improvisation, listening to other characters (in other words, "*re*acting" instead of acting), script analysis, and organic physical work. As much as anything else, learning Meisner helped me to "be in the moment," and I learned how to truly respond to what's happening in a scene instead of just "performing" what I think will work best. (Hope that makes sense.) It made my acting infinitely more realistic and believable and took what talent I had to a whole new level.

So, armed with my newfound skills, I went to more auditions. And got turned down. I went to *more* auditions, and got called back for some parts…only to be rejected again. I'd hit that dreaded wall. It was unbelievably disheartening not knowing when (or even *if*) I'd work again. The instability was downright scary, truth be told. I never knew when my next paycheck was coming. I couldn't go on any vacations, either, because

a) I couldn't afford it, and b) I needed to stay in town and be available for auditions. I put my head down and kept after it…but it played utter hell on my psyche. I partied a lot to help me forget about it, but I sorely needed some type of therapy. Problem was, I just couldn't afford that either.

Then, just when I was reaching my lowest point, I re-discovered a beautiful form of psychic healing, one that I'd learned as a child: hiking. But now I added another element to it: screaming.

I was living in Marina del Rey, I remember, when a couple of buddies of mine—also struggling actors— invited me to go for a run with them up Temescal Canyon, a long, rising gorge with a beautiful hiking trail in Topanga State Park, on the western edge of the city. (And it may or may not be a coincidence that Temescal is only a mile or so from the home in which we currently live.) So I went, and when we got to the top of the canyon, all of Los Angeles—my gigantic, gorgeous, cruel city—was spread out beneath us. It was quite an inspirational and revelatory moment.

I went back there by myself a week or two later. And when I got to the top this time, I gazed upon that beautiful panorama for a few moments; then out of nowhere, a long, miserable scream erupted from…well, from my soul, really. "AAAAAAAAAHHH!!!" That one felt great, so I let 'er rip with several more. As I yelled, I could almost physically feel all the pain, anguish, and disappointment leaving my body. (Hippy-dippy stuff, I know, but it's true.) I screamed myself hoarse, then made my way back down to my Jeep.

On that return trip, I felt more at peace than I had in a long time.

And over the next couple or three years, *that* was my therapy. Practically every week—I usually went on Friday or Saturday—I'd drive to Topanga State Park, stow my truck, and then make my way up. Once I got up there, I'd let Los Angeles have it. (Occasionally I'd have to stop while other hikers passed by looking at me with confusion or fear.) But I would scream at the casting directors, at the producers, at all the people who'd said no to me that week. It was my way of dealing with the *un*fairness, the *in*justice, and the *wrong*ness of my job. And it worked beautifully. Unfortunately, I had numerous letdowns during that period, so my screaming was plenty warranted. Here are some memorable examples:

I read several times for a role in a film called *The Rainmaker*, which was directed by Francis Ford Coppola. It had an incredible cast—Matt Damon, Danny DeVito, Jon Voight, et. al—and I read for Cliff, the abusive husband of Claire Danes's character. For a while, everybody wanted me for the role. "He's our guy, he's our guy"…then at the last minute, Coppola cast Andrew Shue as Cliff. It crushed me.

From the top of Temescal Canyon, I screamed at Coppola for a good three minutes, and informed him that he couldn't direct his way out of a grocery sack. Then it was on to the next.

I was also really close to getting the part of Cushman in *Jerry Maguire*. It was between Jerry O'Connell and me; Cameron Crowe, the writer/director, was also a Seattle guy, so I was hoping with all my heart he'd give it to the hometown boy. And as you probably already know, O'Connell got the role. That broke my heart.

From the top of Temescal Canyon, I lustily made Cameron Crowe aware of my hope that his little football movie completely tanked. Then it was on to the next.

There were plenty of other disappointments, but those two are first on the list. And through it all, The Top of Temescal Canyon—which I just now realized would make a great folk song title—kept me from simply giving up. I was learning to live with disappointment, something of which Vincent Chase would've been extremely proud.

I toiled on. And slowly but surely, things started going my way. That next year, I was cast in several TV shows, produced a movie, and really started to understand my business. It was time to level up.

Chapter 5:
Success? You Be the Judge

(Oct. 5)

Tonight, after the kids go to bed, Sharon and I plan to watch a little TV.

We've DVR'ed a show on CBS called *Code Black*, which is a hospital drama in the vein of *ER*. I've never seen it, but I'll be watching this episode with interest (and a little trepidation, too), because I have a guest-starring role in it.

In all honesty, I'm not really looking forward to it. I've done at least fifty guest-star spots on TV shows, and though I watch them when they air, I'm inevitably disappointed by them. I always second-guess my performance—"Oh, I should've done this, I should've played that differently," etcetera—and a lot of my screen time is invariably edited out. (I understand that that has to happen because of time constraints, but it still sucks.) So I've never, even back when I was first starting out, been able to enjoy watching myself on TV.

That said, the episode shoot was an enjoyable one. I play a soccer coach and dad whose team bus crashes, and through the course of the episode we find out that my character's son — the team's star player — has to have his injured leg amputated. So there was a whole gamut of emotions that I got to play, and most of my scenes were with Rob Lowe, which was cool. Plus, as an athletic guy and a father in real life, I was a perfect fit for the part. (It was right in my Wiehl-house, in other words. Haha.) So, barring any editing heavy-handedness, it should be a nice little spot for me.

Doing these guest-star roles is kind of a mixed bag. The main reason I do them is to pay the bills. And my main job with these roles is to support the show's stars and make them look good (I compare it to being an offensive lineman in football, whose objective is to help ensure the success of the "position players"—the quarterback, running backs, etc.). It's kind of an "all guts, no glory" thing. And doing so is sort of bittersweet, because part of me—the part with the big ego that's common to most every actor—thinks that *I* should be one of the stars. The feeling is even stronger when I remember that there was a time when I *was* one of them. (And we'll get to that.) What's humbling, what puts it all in perspective and tells my ego to pipe the hell down, is realizing that I'm blessed to be able to have a role—even a relatively small one—on a national TV show in the first place. There aren't a lot of people who can support themselves for twenty-plus years as a Hollywood actor, and I'm extremely fortunate to have done so.

*Un*fortunately, these past couple of years have really been the least lucrative of my career. Part of that is because of *Devil's Dolls*, which for now I have to put in the loss column. We're trying to mount a grass-roots social media campaign for it, but I'm not sure how much help that will be. And truth be told, though social media is the way of the world these days, I'm not too hip on it. I just opened an Instagram account this morning, and all it's done so far is confuse the heck out of me.

But I'll keep going. Hopefully, this *Code Black* episode and the social media stuff (once I figure it out) will create some sorely-needed buzz in what's a pretty stagnant point in my career. So go ahead and say it with me:

It's on to the next.

And as you'll see, I've had to move "on to the next" in a variety of ways.

* * * *

Dammit, if nobody's going to hire me, well, I'll just hire myself.

In the midst of that dry work spell I had, that thought became a frequent one, and by about mid-'96 I'd set things in motion to make it a reality. There was a guy named Gene Bernard whom I'd met in my Barron/Brown classes; at the time he was working as an editor for *Entertainment Tonight* (and has since gone on to have a successful career as a director, most notably on daytime shows like *Rachael Ray* and *The Queen Latifah Show*), but was taking acting classes with his wife so they could learn more about the business. Gene told me he had an early draft of a screenplay about a washed-up baseball pitcher who gets involved in a crime caper—it was kind of a *Lock, Stock and Two Smoking Barrels*-meets-Coen Brothers kind of thing, and I loved it. Furthermore, I could perfectly see myself playing the lead role. We started collaborating on a script revision, and though originally the story was set in the South, I talked him into changing the setting to Yakima, my hometown. The change in locale suggested a perfect title for it too:

Yakima Wash. Setting (and filming) the movie there would be great because we could scout locations and get housing for the cast/crew for free. Once that was decided, we did some fundraising to finance the film; we raised about $60,000 to pay for equipment, travel, and for one meal a day for everybody. I really didn't have much of an idea about how to produce a film, but I was sort of forced to learn quickly; I now think of my experience working on that movie as my "unofficial" film grad school.

We had a fantastic cast. Ritchie Montgomery, Vyto Ruginis, Kevin Weisman, lots of terrific character actors who brought some great spirit to the film. Thankfully, the actors all agreed to "SAG deferred" pay, meaning they would make money if/when the film was sold to a distributor, but got nothing up front; in reality, getting SAG deferments means that actually getting paid is a bit of a long shot, and actors often agree to do the project because they like the script and the filmmakers. We also had M.C. Gainey as our heavy. M.C. had been working in Hollywood since the late 70s, and it was great to have veterans like him and Vyto as part of the team. Since Gene Bernard already knew the film so well—I mean, c'mon, he wrote it!—he directed, I played the lead, and we shot the movie over six weeks or so in the summer of '97. It was a fantastic (if incredibly nerve-wracking) experience. My parents housed about ten people at a time, and family friends hosted the cast members as they came and went. And we couldn't afford film dailies (the nightly sessions where the director and producers review the unedited footage shot each day), so we had "weeklies." Every weekend my dad would drive the raw film over to Seattle, where Gene, the other producers and I would go over the preceding week's scenes. At the same time, we were scouting locations for the next week, troubleshooting any problems we had, *and* still raising money to finance the post-production. It was Producing-By-the-Seat-of-Your-Pants 101.

But we finished it. And it's a fun ride. Gene edited it, and we got through most of the post-production work on it. But unfortunately, no one bought the film, so it's sitting on the shelf collecting dust.

Even so, it was a remarkable learning experience for me. For one thing, as the lead actor, I really learned what it took to put a film on my back, so to speak. But in a larger sense, I learned *so*, so much about the filmmaking business. I mean, we made a movie from scratch! Doing that gave me first-hand, boots-on-the-ground knowledge about the amount of work that goes into producing a film.

And probably the most valuable lesson I learned, one that has stayed with me ever since, was about the casting process. The lesson was this: *the people doing the casting really want you, the actor, to succeed.* That realization came to me as we were casting *Yakima Wash.* We had so much to do, so many loose ends to tie up, that we really hoped that each actor would come in, nail the audition, and we could cast them and move on. I'd always thought that casting directors were just out to get you. And it was an epiphany to realize that hey, they want to find somebody for the role—and that's often as critical to them as booking the role is to the actor.

Realizing that took a lot of pressure off for me. It reinforced the concept of acting as a business. And once that pressure was lessened, my auditions improved dramatically. Plus, once I'd proved to myself that I could successfully make a movie, I started worrying even less about auditions. Because if no one else would cast me, I'd just cast myself in my own movie. It gave me sort of an "I don't give a shit" attitude—which translated to a *huge* amount of confidence. And that trust led to a lot of success.

* * * *

I mentioned "leveling up" earlier, right? Well, that pretty much defines 1997 and '98 for me. I did I think five guest stars in '97, including a great episode in the final season of the NBC sitcom *Wings*. But the guest-starring role that I remember most from that year, the one that I think caught a lot of people's eyes, was in the fifth episode of a new show called *Buffy the Vampire Slayer*. I played Owen, the love interest of Sarah Michelle Gellar's Buffy, and the episode's storyline centered around our relationship; the show was just starting to create a buzz amongst young viewers—TV's saintly demographic—and I had several powerful scenes. Plus, I got to work with some big-name people. I was creeping toward that inner circle of working Hollywood actors.

(A quick sidelight: I think it was in '97 that I played Horny Guy. Haha. Let me explain: I auditioned for one of the leads in *Can't Hardly Wait*, a teen comedy film starring Jennifer Love Hewitt. My first read went well, so they narrowed it down to me and a couple other guys, and I did a screen test with Love Hewitt. And I saw that they were also casting a bit part for a character simply known as Horny Guy. So I told the casting directors with a big cheeky grin, "Hey, if I don't get this lead, can I play Horny Guy?" And sure enough, the lead part—Love Hewitt's character's boyfriend—went to another actor. But they called me and asked me if I was serious about playing Horny Guy, to which I responded that I *absolutely* was. So I got to call my parents and boast about the wonderful new film role I'd gotten: Horny Guy. Now back to your regularly scheduled reading.)

Anyway: early the next year, I got an express invitation to that inner circle—one that I thought would boost my stardom into overdrive.

My agent and manager teamed up to get me a *gigantic* audition. It was for one of the leads in the pilot of an edgy, hard-hitting new show called *Bronx County*, which centered around a group of attorneys in NYC. The content would be gritty and raw, and it was to be *the* big hit of the next season for CBS. It had some powerful people behind it, too. It was being produced by guys like

Barry Schindel, who would go on to be a great showrunner for *Law & Order*, among other things; John Sacret Young, who'd produced *China Beach* (and would eventually be a *West Wing* showrunner); and even Sydney Pollack, who was…hell, Sydney Pollack. Plus it would be directed by Thomas Carter, who at the time was Hollywood's newest directorial darling.

I think there were six of us doing screen tests for the role, which seemed like a lot—but hey, it was for a lead in a big-name show, so what the heck. The way these auditions work for most network shows is that first you have several auditions, with the casting director and then for one or more of the producers (which I'd already done). Then if they like you, they call you in for a screen test at the production studio (which was Paramount, in this case). Then, if you make *that* cut, you test again for the network within a day or so. I remember driving to Paramount that morning being nervous as all get-out, and I went into this dark room and worked with John Young and Thomas Carter for a while. Then I went into another room and did the test, with all the important guys— Young, Carter, Sydney Pollack, everybody—watching every move I made.

And I crushed it. I know I did so for two reasons (well, three actually, but here are two for now): Sydney Pollack told me so, and I was able to get my tie off.

Apparently, the tie was the audition's litmus test. When they were working with me beforehand, Thomas Carter told me, "Listen, kid, in the scene, the script calls for you to rip your tie off. So if you need to loosen it ahead of time or whatever, do what you can to make that happen." During my test, I was able to do it in one pretty fluid motion; I found out later that some of the other guys hadn't been so lucky. (And isn't it weird how one seemingly minor, inconsequential task could mean so much?) In any case, my scene must've gone well, because on my way out the door, Sydney Pollack leaned over and said, "Hey, kid, nice job." I was pumped for sure.

And that third reason I knew it went well? They called me within an hour or two and asked me to go to CBS that afternoon and test again. So I did so, with a quick drive home beforehand to choke down a sandwich. (I remember not being hungry at all, but I knew that giving such an important audition on an empty stomach would *not* be a good idea. I mean, fainting in front of network executives would lessen my chances of getting the role. Obviously.)

Testing at CBS is weird, because you usually do it in this dark theater that's down in the basement of one of the buildings. I remember walking down the steps, and my nerves were just going haywire. And it's at times like these that I always try to remember what Kevin Costner's character said in the movie *For the Love of the Game,* when he played a major-league pitcher:

Clear the mechanism.

Shut everything else out and focus on the task at hand. Try to center all your attention on what you are about to do. Quiet your mind. Fixate. Concentrate. Breathe slowly…steadily…get in The Zone.

Listen to your breaths.

And then…eventually…

You're ready.

That day at CBS, I walked into that room, and I *gave them the character.* And that's important when you get to that point in the process of an audition as big as that one. When you just do a regular audition, it's like an artist using a large brush to fling paint at a canvas. You hope something meaningful happens, but you're just taking shots in the dark, pretty much. But doing a screen test for a network is a lot more refined because by that point you've had a lot more time with the material. It's like adding the last brush strokes to a Picasso work. After your test, you want the network execs to say, "*That's* the character we want in this show."

If memory serves, that day was a Friday. (That Monday, I remember, was a holiday—Martin Luther King, Jr. Day of '98.) I knew there was one other actor who had the best shot of anyone at getting the role—a guy named Michael Vartan, who was another rising star at the time—who was flying in from New York for the audition. So I knew we'd have to wait for him to do his test to find out who got the part.

On Monday, Holly Lebed called. I answered—I'd been able to upgrade to a sleek, less-clunky cell by then—and she was somehow laughing and crying at the same time. "You got it," she croaked. "You *got* it! *Bronx County*! You GOT IT!!!" I flipped. We all went out that night: me, my girlfriend Eryn (who…well, more on her in a minute), Holly, some other agents from J. Michael Bloom (Holly's agency), my manager Mark, and my roommate Billy. I remember feeling on top of the stinkin' *world*. I'd gotten a lead on not just a TV show, but what was going to be the big hit of the next season. Press tours, plenty of big job offers coming my way…heck. Even a *TV Guide* cover wasn't out of the realm of possibility. I mean, this was a big, big show.

We shot the pilot in New York that March, and it was *great*. Thomas Carter was a fantastic director. John Sacret Young? One of the best producers I've ever worked with. The whole shoot was phenomenal. And the hits just kept coming. I remember John Young calling me while they were doing post-production and saying, "Listen: we want to give you the 'and' card." (You know how the opening credits of a show name the main actors? Those name credits are called "cards," i.e. first card, second card, and so on. It's always done in order of importance. And the "and" card is always last, and is generally given to the cast member with the most Hollywood seniority.) Some of the other cast members— like Alan Rosenberg, for example, who'd already had a long run on *L.A. Law*, among other things—had much more extensive acting resumes than I did at the time. So for the producers to want to give me the "and" credit was tremendous, because it would signify that I had a lot of industry clout. "Kid, you're gonna be the star of this thing," John Young promised. In essence, they were grooming me to be one of the focal points of the show. It was fantastic.

Let me back up a bit: when I was auditioning for (and then shooting the pilot of) *Bronx County*, I was also helping with pre-production of my own second movie, a teenage vampire flick called *Cold Hearts*. This one had a bigger budget than *Yakima Wash*, and was a more expansive production overall. I had one of the leads, and was a producer; we were scheduled to shoot it that May in New Jersey. So I was in Ocean City, a beach town just south of Atlantic City, in the midst of shooting a movie, when the 1998/99 Fall TV lineups were announced. I figured *Bronx County* would be put on the CBS schedule for a nine- or ten o'clock weeknight slot.

It was the second or third week of May, and I remember waking up the day of the new lineup announcements thinking, "Today is gonna be *awesome*." Though I wasn't acting in any scenes that day, I would be monitoring the shoot as a producer; I also knew that I'd have to make a quick trip up to NYC after the announcement to be on hand for the official *Bronx*

County press briefing. (One of the producers was to call me on my cell the moment the announcement was made so I could book a charter flight from Jersey.) It probably goes without saying that I was super-excited for what the next couple of days had in store.

As the morning passed, I didn't get a call. We broke for lunch, and *still* no call. I started getting nervous. Then, late in the afternoon, by which time I was nearly jumping out of my skin, my phone rang. It was Thomas Carter, the director…and it was the worst news I could've imagined. "Sorry, kid. We're not on the lineup," he said. "Maybe mid-season, but no promises for that, either."

What???

I…I just couldn't comprehend it. It was…this show was the next big hit. Wha…*why*??? As I eventually found out, the show was considered *too* edgy for CBS, so they passed on it. Remember, this was back in the 1990s—years before cable and streaming networks raised the bar on racy content—and the Big Four networks still preferred softer, less obtrusive shows. I remember that CBS touted a different new show called *L.A. Doctors* as its "edgy new drama." Problem was, the show was about as edgy as a bowl of lime Jello, apparently, and was canceled after one season. *C'est la vie.* But thinking about it now, I believe that *Bronx County* was simply ahead of its time; I think it would be a big success if it premiered now.

I recall going out and getting hammered that night. I mean, I was feeling pretty damn low. I would say that I threw myself headlong into my work, but in all honesty, the entire experience of shooting *Cold Hearts* was awful too. We had a first-time director, a pretty crappy script, and a bunch of young actors who turned out to be pains in our collective asses. It *was* picked up, actually, and played on Showtime a few times, but…the movie was just a train wreck. The day we wrapped shooting was a huge relief. The most important lesson I learned from the whole *Cold Hearts* ordeal was what *not* to do when you make a movie.

So the *Bronx County* tragedy just crushed me. It wasn't all bad though: I'd done a nice job in the pilot, apparently, because CBS offered me a development deal, meaning they would agree to cast me in another drama pilot the next season. At the same time, some NBC execs who'd also seen the *Bronx County* pilot made me a counter-offer, hoping I'd do a comedy series for them. In the end, I decided to stick with CBS, mainly because I preferred drama to comedy, and I just felt more loyal to CBS since they'd already shown faith in me. But having some career choices was a good thing.

And *another* good thing about having your hopes stomped on: it's fuel for the fire, baby. I'm not sure whether it was the added confidence of being cast in a major pilot, or anger at not having the show picked up, or just the simple desperation of really needing a job…whatever the reason, the intensity of my auditions rose to a nearly feverous pitch. And that newfound passion got me results: I was cast as a guest star in several TV shows, most notably in a recurring role as a fighter pilot in *Pensacola: Wings of Gold,* a syndicated drama about pilots at a Naval Air Station in Florida. 1998, this was, and doing that show was a ton of fun; it starred James Brolin as the squadron commander, and we shot down in San Diego. I played Lt. Stanley "Swamp" Langdon, a pilot from Louisiana, and I did six episodes altogether. I would've done more, but I knew I'd need to be available for the upcoming pilot season, since CBS had promised (and paid me, haha) to cast me in a pilot that next go-round.

Speaking of that CBS money: I'd used some of the development deal cash to buy a house in West L.A., and my girlfriend Eryn and I had moved into it together. We'd met at a bar in Manhattan Beach, and by the time I bought the house, I'd fallen hard for her. She'd been working in advertising at Fox Studios, but I think she got all starry-eyed believing she was dating the next Hollywood icon; she'd quit her job at Fox to go to Jersey with us to shoot *Cold Hearts*. (She had a bit part in it, and was…Wardrobe Assistant, maybe? Some minor crew job.) In any case, we were totally in love. I thought she was the one. And she, in turn, believed I was Superman to her Lois Lane.

So pilot season rolls around, and CBS cast me in the pilot of a show called *Partners,* a drama about the personal lives of a group of Bay Area cops. I played a young attorney, and the cast also had Piper Laurie, Bonnie Bedelia, Amanda Peet, and Marg Helgenberger (who, interestingly enough, was married at the time to Alan Rosenberg, whom I'd worked with on *Bronx County* the year before). We shot the pilot in the Oakland area, and I remember everybody saying the *exact same things* about it that I'd heard one year before. "Oh, the show is great…we're the darlings of CBS…we're guaranteed to get picked up …" *Shit. Here we go again.*

And my dreaded assumptions were correct. The lineup announcement day comes, and no call…no call…then by the end of the day, I realize there's not going to *be* a call. *Partners* didn't make the fall lineup. *DAMMIT.*

I drove to the store and bought a twelve-pack of beer, and I went and sat on the roof of my garage and drank the whole damn thing. When Eryn got home from work—she'd started picking up shifts as a bartender— she came up there. And despite my full-on inebriation, I'll never forget our conversation.

"Hey. What's up?" she asked when she finished climbing the steps. "Did you hear anything?"

I just stared at her drunkenly for a moment. "Yeah," I finally said. "We didn't get picked up."

"Oh." She stared at me for a few seconds, and in her face, I saw a totally new expression: disappointment. Maybe even a little disgust. As the silence spun out, I could almost hear myself tumbling off her mental pedestal. We just faced each other, her eyes averted in discomfort.

"What if ..." I could barely bring myself to say the words. "What if I don't make it?"

"Yeah." It seemed like Eryn, in turn, could hardly bear to hear them. "What if ...?" I don't think she'd ever considered that. But once it got in her head, there it stayed. From the moment she left the garage roof that night, she was a different person.

Not that I was around to see it. A few weeks later she left me for another guy. It tore...me...up. I remember that my mom came down and spent some time with me, and Lis visited too. I was brokenhearted. Mom said at one point, "You just need to go take a walk." Huh. A *walk?* I did her one better: I recall that as my Forrest Gump period. I started running, and running...I mean, I didn't grow a beard or anything, but I'd run twelve, fifteen miles at a stretch. Rather than run away from the pain, I was trying to run it *off.* In the meantime, my auditions? They got even better. I was just *raw.* I did an audition for *Touched by an Angel* where I read for the part of a Vietnam vet, and though I didn't get it, it was the best audition I've ever done. Pure, unfettered emotion.

And right around this time, at a point when I felt like my life was in complete disarray, we had our ten-year high school reunion. Remember me talking a while back about the agreement I'd made with my friend during our junior year? About how we both thought we'd do something important as adults, and we'd compare notes at our ten-year reunion? That indeed happened, and it was truly a revelatory experience.

It was late summer, '99, and I went up to Yakima still depressed over Eryn dumping me. I went to the thing, and a lot of my former classmates were like, "Hey, it's Chris Wiehl! Superstar!" That kind of stuff. Problem was, I didn't feel like a star at all…I just felt sad. Sure, I'd been on a lot of TV shows, done huge commercials, shot a movie right there in Yakima a year or two before. But did I feel like a success? Far from it.

I saw my friend, and the first thing she said to me was, "Well, looks like you won the bet." (Though we'd never actually made a "bet," I knew exactly what she meant.) Turns out she'd married her high school sweetheart, and they had two kids; they both had steady jobs, and she and her family seemed to have comparatively simple (and extremely *stable*) lives. She said she was happy, and looked it.

"I don't know if I won the bet or not," I told her. "I mean, I've done all these shows, movies, I'm working all the time…but am I *happy*? I'm not. I just got my heart broken. And you—you've got a great family, a great job. You're happy. And to me, that's success. *That's* doing something important."

We decided we'd let it ride till the twenty-year reunion, then see where we were then. But that conversation with my friend was a revealing one. And as you'll see, the tides eventually turned somewhat for both of us.

But for me, both in work and life, great things were on the horizon.

Chapter 6:
Making Plays

(Oct. 11)

You're probably wondering why I say "On to the next" so much, right? As I mentioned a while back, it's something I picked up from my agent Dan Baron; it might help to explain it in a little more detail, and I figure since we're at it, I'll give you the general history of the people who've represented me. Goodness knows, I wouldn't have a career without them!

Dan has been my agent for the majority of my twenty-three years in the business. Right from the beginning, he would always be thinking about my next audition, role, etcetera, even if I was in the midst of another one. He told me that sort of forward-thinking mentality was a necessity for both him *and* me—that instead of wasting time trying to figure out why I *didn't* get a part, it was better to focus on the future. It was better to invest my time and energy on *things I could control* (there it is again), like preparing as best I could to audition for parts I still had a shot at booking. "I mean, you don't talk about all the girls who said no to you, right?" he told me once. "Of course you don't. It's on to next girl…on to the next job…on to the next." (And the way he actually speaks the words is beautiful. It sort of rolls out of his mouth; spelled phonetically, it's "AHNNN du-thu-NEXXXTTT…" I love it.)

Dan first represented me—well, let me give you the full history of my representation: Holly Lebed, you may remember, was my agent in NYC; she continued representing me when I first got to L.A. She, along with two others named Zoe Lieberman and Mark Armstrong, were my representatives at an agency called HWA. After two or three years, Mark left HWA to become a talent manager. (FYI, the difference between a manager and an agent is that a manager helps an actor with his or her career in general. The manager helps with auditions, yes, but also with scheduling, publicity, all sorts of stuff; it's much more personal. An agent's main purpose, meanwhile, is to help the actor find gigs.) I was one of Mark's first managerial clients, and the agent who replaced him at HWA was Dan Baron, so he started representing me too.

A few years after that, Dan, Holly, and Zoe moved to the J. Michael Bloom Agency; I followed them and stayed with Bloom for several more years. (By this time, Mark was my full-time manager.) Then Bloom folded and all the agents scattered, so I had a guy named Jason Gutman as an agent for a while. (He was with an agency called Gersh.) And though Jason was great, and did a lot for me, he worked out of New York. I wanted somebody here in L.A. as my "point" agent. So I called up Dan Baron—this would've been in about '06, I guess—who by then was with Agency for the Performing Arts here in town; I asked him if he'd represent me again, he agreed, and I've been with Dan and APA ever since.

Whew! So that's that. I've been extremely blessed to have fantastic representation my whole career. Dan, Holly, and my manager Mark have all done great things for me. Most of all, they've kept me sane. They've kept my nose to the grindstone. They've stayed with me when things didn't look good, either professionally or personally. And when I thought I might die—both literally and figuratively—they stuck with me too. And for that, I owe them huge debts of gratitude.

On to the next.

* * * *

There are two cliché sayings that sort of sum up the turn of the millennium for me. Take your pick: "Time heals all wounds," and "what doesn't kill you makes you stronger."

For two years in a row, I was a lead in a big network pilot, and neither of those pilots were picked up. Right on the heels of that, the woman I loved dumped me. And then I had an immensely enlightening conversation at my reunion, one that really got me thinking about what was important to me. Add all that together, and it put me in a space of…I don't know. Rawness? Openness? I was ripe for change, I'll say that. And to paraphrase Dylan, changes were a'comin'.

In early June of '99, I think, I auditioned for a lead in *another* network drama pilot. The show was *Bull*, and it was about a group of Wall Street investment bankers who go rogue to start their own firm. It was a Warner Brothers show and was created by Michael Chernuchin, a titan producer of shows like *Law & Order, 24*, and tons more. I auditioned for that at Warner Brothers, then read again for the director, then did a screen test for Peter Roth, the WB president. And here are the results, in order, of those auditions: nailed it, brilliant read, crushed it again. (And I jokingly told Peter Roth I'd wash his car if he'd give me a part.) My last screen test was for TNT, the cable network that eventually aired the show, and I knocked that one out of the park too.

I got one of the leads. And I still owe Peter Roth a car wash. (Mr. Roth, if you're reading this, feel free to give me a call, and I'll gladly come settle up my end of the bargain.) I got the part of Carson Boyd, one of the investment bankers, and I joined some great actors in the cast like Alicia Coppola, Stanley Tucci, George Newbern, and others. Warner Brothers was terrific, because they took me in "second position." Here's what that meant: though *Partners* hadn't been picked up in May, CBS still owned me for several months in case they decided to run it as a mid-season replacement or something. So WB cast me even though there was a chance they couldn't air the *Bull* pilot with me in it if CBS decided to air the *Partners* one. (I hope that makes sense. And acting contracts are different now, but back then being put in second position was fairly common.) In the end, everything worked out, as *Partners* never aired, and *Bull* aired without a problem after CBS released me from my contract.

TNT picked up the show, and I was stoked. It was the network's first original series, right around the time that cable networks in general—TNT, AMC, FX, etcetera—began featuring original programming. We shot the first twenty-two episodes, and I really developed as an actor during that season. And then, halfway through Season 1, TNT canceled it. And I've since learned that it wasn't really the show itself that was at fault. Right as we premiered, the *real* Wall Street was sort of in crisis mode, as the tech boom that had raised the Dow Jones Average for the previous few years was going bust. And because of that, the TNT execs—who apparently understood the stock market far better than I did—felt like nobody wanted to watch a show about affluent Wall Street bankers. Whatever the case, they axed us after eleven episodes.

But at that point, after having my hopes already dashed more than once in recent years, I took it in stride. It was painful, yes, but much less so than the *Bronx County* and *Partners* tragedies. (And it was great having a steady paycheck!) And then, of course, it was on to the next.

And luckily, "the next" wasn't far off. Within just a few weeks, I was cast in the pilot of *First Monday*, a CBS show about Supreme Court Justices. *Unbelievable* cast: Joe Mantegna, James Garner, and Charles Durning played some of the justices—there was some incredible talent. (I got to play Jerry, Joe Mantegna's character's clerk, so practically all my scenes were with him.) And it was created by Donald Bellisario, who'd already been the creator for *Magnum P.I., JAG, Quantum Leap*, and others. We were a lock, right?

Right?

Well…sheesh. Here's what happened: the May lineup announcement day came, and I got no call in the morning. No call by lunch. *Great. Not AGAIN?!* Then, mid-afternoon, Don Bellisario finally called and said we'd be picked up as a mid-season replacement, meaning *First Monday* would premiere in January and replace a show that had been canceled. It wasn't as good, as we wouldn't have nearly as big a rollout as a Fall premiere, but hey, it was a pickup nonetheless. And I found out later that we were lucky to have been picked up at all. Turns out that Don Bellisario had to make a last-minute flight to New York to talk Les Moonves, the president of CBS, into putting us on the schedule.

But then some wacky scheduling, along with a simple offhand joke by David Letterman, basically doomed us. The pilot premiered on a Tuesday, right after *JAG*, but CBS put us on the weekly schedule on Fridays—and as many folks know, Friday night is where TV shows go to die. And then, just a couple hours after the pilot aired on a Tuesday in mid-January of '02 (with the next episode scheduled for that Friday, and each subsequent episode every Friday thereafter), David Letterman told a joke about it. It was something like: "Did anybody watch the *First Monday* premiere tonight? Let's see: the show is *First Monday*...but it aired on a Tuesday...and it's going to be shown every Friday. Is anybody else confused?" When he said that, we knew we were screwed.

And we were. Our ratings were pretty low, and we were canceled after only thirteen episodes. The experience was fantastic while it lasted—I mean, I got to work daily with some of the best actors in the business—but my luck was just *crappy*, man. On the one hand, I was constantly working, and my resume was getting pretty big—but once, just *once*, I would've loved to do a show that lasted more than one season. I didn't feel like that was too much to ask.

A few months later, I heard that ESPN would soon be casting for its first original scripted drama, about the lives of some fictitious pro football players. The show was called *Playmakers*, and it was a game-changer.

* * * *

During the *First Monday* run, short-lived though it was, I had the distinction of being on two CBS shows at once. I did a couple of episodes of the second season of *CSI* (the original one, set in Las Vegas); it was right when the show was exploding in popularity, and it was the number-one drama on TV at the time, so it was great to have a big audience like that. I played a medic—I think his name was Hank—and apparently they liked my character, so they asked me to come back and do a few more episodes the next season. I got to be part of a great story arc in which Hank has a turbulent relationship with Jorja Fox's character. It was a cool experience, and I was sad to see it end.

Sometime in late 2002, I heard through the grapevine that ESPN was planning to create its first scripted show, about the behind-the-scenes goings-on of a fictional pro football team. That really sparked my interest, both because of my build—I'm 6'3', about 195—and my supreme interest in football (Go Seahawks!). I thought being on a show like that would be an absolute blast, and that I'd be perfect for it. So I bugged my manager Mark about it, and he finally got me a script for the pilot. Meantime, I expressed my interest in the show to my agents at Gersh, and after a little investigating they came back and advised me *not* to pursue it. The pay would be terrible, they said; if I were to get a lead role on the show, I'd take about a seventy-percent pay cut from my previous work on *First Monday, Bull*, etcetera.

I told them I wanted to try for it anyway. I'd read the script and thought the writing was just sensational; plus, being part of a show like that wasn't about the money in the first place. I was (and am still) an athlete, and being on a show about football meant…we'd be playing a lot of football. It was *exactly* the kind of physically challenging role I wanted (and needed, honestly).

So my agents acquiesced, and Jason Gutman set me up with an audition. I really wanted to play Derek McConnell, the quarterback; the part fit my type and build, and I thought I could nail it. So the casting directors had me work up a long monologue of Derek's, and I went in and read for creator/executive producer John Eisendrath. And it went very, very well. *So* well, in fact, that they called my manager the next day and said, "Listen, we don't want Chris to play the quarterback— that's not a very big part. We'd rather have him as Olczyk, the linebacker. That's the biggest part on the show, and we'd rather have Chris play him." So I went back in to meet with some of the producers and writers, and in a nutshell, they told me that Olczyk would be the star of the show, and they wanted me for it. I said that I just didn't have the build to believably play a pro linebacker.

"Well," one of them said, "what if we make Olczyk a defensive back instead?"

"Listen," I said. "If I play Derek McConnell, and *I do my job*, Olczyk may be the star now…but in all the seasons after this first one, the star will be Derek McConnell."

Silence filled the room, and I knew I'd sold them. That sort of swagger, I think, was exactly what they were looking for. And they called me a little bit later and told me I would play Derek McConnell in the first season of *Playmakers*. (Insert the *Rocky* theme reprise.)

That was in early April of '03. I was told we'd need to be in Toronto in late May to begin shooting, so I had about six weeks to become a pro quarterback. Yeah. I immediately started training like a professional athlete…and alllll those years I'd played sports as a kid were suddenly invaluable. I had a guy named Thomas Roe, who still trains me from time to time, work with me; in addition to all the running, foot drills, and weightlifting, he trained me for several hours each day on how to more accurately throw a football. Doing that is quite different from throwing a baseball, which is what I was used to; you grip the ball differently, and the delivery is much quicker. And you release the ball from above your shoulder, right next to your ear, instead of away from your body as you would with a baseball. It definitely took some getting used to, but after a few thousand throws to Thomas, I got the hang of it.

I got to Toronto in May, and right from the get-go the camaraderie was great. Omar Gooding (Cuba's younger brother) and Russell Hornsby played the running backs, Jason Smith was Olczyk the linebacker, and Tony Denison played Coach George—great guys all. The days were long and challenging—on "game day" shoots we'd go for fourteen, fifteen hours, and sometimes I just slept in my trailer instead of going back to my rented condo—but it was unbelievably fulfilling. I mean, we were playing a ton of football! I had a guy named Mike…Mike something…shoot, I can't remember his last name. Mike was my stunt double, and he was a former Canadian Football League quarterback; he worked with me on getting the pro quarterback "look" down. He showed me how to handle the footwork, how to see through the huge linemen (I'm 6'3', but these linemen—a lot of them former CFL players themselves—were 6'6", 6'7") on passing plays, and how to throw like a top-tier quarterback. When I first started training, I could throw the ball maybe twenty-five yards or so, but by the time we finished shooting that first season I was slinging it for fifty on a damn *rope*.

We shot the whole first season in Toronto, so I was there from May until October. I loved the whole atmosphere. It was hard being away from Sarah, the woman I was dating at the time (and eventually married, and...well, more on Sarah in a little bit. *Plenty* more), but I had a great time overall. We shot all the games in Toronto's Skydome, which was cool; I thought it was kind of weird that onscreen, all our games (both home and away) were in domed stadiums, but no one seemed to care, so what the heck. As I said, the rapport amongst the actors was fantastic, and there was a fraternal, incredibly team-like mentality on set and off.

All that said, probably the greatest thing about being involved with *Playmakers* was the fantastic writing. The show writers—John Eisendrath, Peter Egan, Stephen Hootstein, some others—came up with storylines for the players that were both dramatic and incredibly relevant: steroid use, of course, but also spousal abuse, homosexuality in pro athletes...a lot of topics that have come to the forefront in the *real* NFL (and in pro sports in general) in recent years. The show was undoubtedly ahead of its time; I think the writers had amazing foresight in tackling issues that had yet to be addressed (or even *known,* for that matter) in real-life sports.

So we shot the season there in Toronto, and we were so busy we didn't really have time to pay attention to anything else—it was like we were living in a bubble, almost. After we had finished, Sarah met me in Toronto, and she and I took a train ride down to NYC, where we had dinner with my sister Lis (she was living there by that time*)*, then over to Washington, D.C. so Sarah could go to her ten-year high school reunion. That was early October. *Playmakers* had premiered on ESPN in August and was airing every Tuesday night. And totally unbeknownst to me, it was a big hit. All during the train rides, at dinner with Lis, and heck, just walking down the *street*, people were like, "Hey, it's the quarterback!" or "Look! McConnell!" When we got to Sarah's reunion, some of her classmates wanted to talk to me about the show. And listen: I can lie and say I took that sort of instant celebrity in stride…but shoot, I loved it. Most of all, I was glad to know that people were *watching* the damn thing. That meant good ratings, and good ratings would equal show longevity.

When we finally got back to California, and I had a chance to breathe a little bit, I realized the show was creating a pretty good buzz, both for its edgy storylines and its sports appeal. It seemed like we had that magic combination of viewer interest and critical praise—a combo that pretty much ensured our being on ESPN for multiple seasons. I heard rumors that the NFL (and its team owners in particular) hated the show, as it cast the real-life players in a pretty bad light, but I wasn't surprised. And then, in February the American Film Institute named *Playmakers* one of its Top Ten TV Programs of the Year for 2003. I was elated. *Playmakers* — a show *I was one of the stars of* — was a success. It was *about damn time.*

Then, two days after *Playmakers* received the AFI Award, ESPN canceled it.

Once again, it all came down to the almighty dollar. ESPN's chief reason for the cancellation, they said, was that they were "concerned about harming our business relationship with the NFL." (In other words, ESPN wanted to continue suckling from the NFL teat.) Apparently, the NFL front-office guys (along with every other person involved with the organization, it seemed like) despised *Playmakers*, and someone from the NFL administration would complain to ESPN about it pretty much every single week. And it's interesting to note that one of the chief complainants was Steve Bornstein, the NFL Vice President of Media — and *former president of ESPN*. I heard that in reality, ESPN (which is owned by Disney-ABC Television) was in the midst of negotiating a new contract with the league for the rights to air games, and the NFL said that if *Playmakers* wasn't immediately canceled, they'd consider taking their business elsewhere. So ESPN, of course, followed the money and axed us.

Look, I know it was a business decision. Still: it was a big, stinkin' pile of bullshit on the NFL's part. It was a case of the almighty NFL *sweeping its problems under the rug*. Why? Because *Playmakers* predicted the future. During our one season, we had a player come out of the closet as gay, another involved in a murder investigation, and numerous instances of spousal abuse. Sound familiar? Our show dealt with issues that have since given the NFL a pretty tarnished reputation. As I write this chapter—it's October of 2016—the league is dealing with the fallout from *another* domestic violence case:

Giants kicker Josh Brown recently admitted to physically abusing his wife. And what did the NFL do about it? They suspended him for one game. In other words, they looked the other way. As much as I love football, I have to say: Shame on you, NFL. Yeah, the *Playmakers* cancellation was business. But it was *bad* business. Not only did it put me (and a lot of other talented people) out of a job, but it set a pretty ugly precedent for the morality (or lack thereof) of an enormous organization. It was the first case of what's become years of bad form.

Wow. Okay, I'll stop preaching now. I moved on from it, but it took a while. And little did I know it at the time, but my life was about to get infinitely more challenging. In the coming years, I would face some life-changing situations—ones that would make the *Playmakers* fiasco seem tiny in comparison.

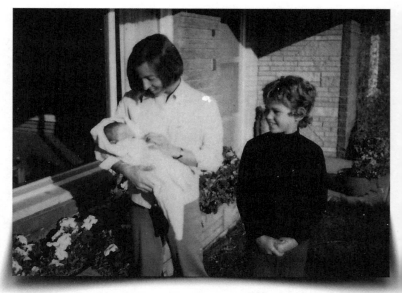

Chris's first Halloween. As his nine-year-old sister Lis looks on, his mother Inga brings two-day-old Chris home from the hospital on Halloween, 1970.

Chris and his mother in 1974.

Chris, at age seven, batting in one of his first baseball games.

Chris, at right, with his longtime friend Brian King during a hike sometime in the early '80s.

Chris, in his senior year of high school, running in a 4x400 relay race.

Chris and his former Yakima Valley Community College drama instructor Dr. George Meschke in December 1996.

Chris in his Jeep as he leaves Yakima to move to Los Angeles in October 1994.

The cast and crew of 1997's "Yakima Wash." Chris is pictured in the top row, holding the "Camp Wiehl Summer '97" sign.

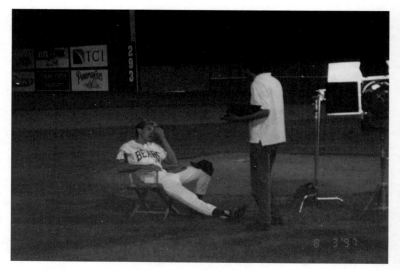

Chris on the set of his self-produced film, "Yakima Wash," in 1997. At right is the film's co-writer/director, Gene Bernard.

Chris with his manager, Mark Armstrong, and his agent, Jason Gutman, at a Halloween party in 1999.

The cover of the New York Times television guide in September 2000, picturing Chris and fellow cast members of "Bull," TNT's first original series.

(Front row) Joe Mantegna, James Garner, Charles Durning
(Back row) Christopher Wiehl, Randy Vasques, Hedy Burress, Joe Flanigan

FIRST MONDAY

Promo shot of CBS's 2002 drama "First Monday." Chris is pictured at the top left.

Chris and the cast of the ESPN series "Playmakers" pictured on the cover of the Los Angeles Times's television guide, just prior to the show's premiere in August 2003.

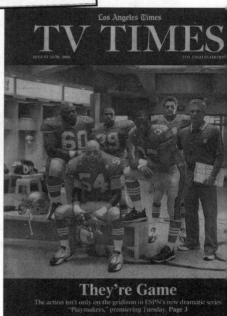

Los Angeles Times
TV TIMES
AUGUST 24-30, 2003   LOS ANGELES EDITION

They're Game
The action isn't only on the gridiron in ESPN's new dramatic series "Playmakers," premiering Tuesday, Page 3

A giant "Playmakers" mural on a building across the street from L.A.'s Staples Center in late 2003. Pictured at right, Chris's head is literally three stories high.

Cavanagh (on the drums) bops around New York City with pals Jason Priestley (left), Larenz Tate and Christopher Wiehl.

Love Monkey
CBS (Tuesdays, 10 p.m., ET)

BY TOM GLIATTO

Maybe Peter Jackson's *King Kong* would have shown more box-office muscle with this title. At any rate, *Love Monkey*, CBS's heavily promoted new hour-long series, comes closest to any recent show in providing the single male primate's answer to *Sex and the City*. Based on a novel by former PEOPLE staffer Kyle Smith, it's a more entertaining, more detailed attempt at constructing a Manhattan fantasy than the Potemkin village on *How I Met Your Mother*. Here we have the city as a playground for thirtysomething men with fun jobs (that they'd just as soon chuck), slim eligible women offering their phone numbers like maidens obliging the gods and a wide range of stomping grounds both uptown and down, bars, basketball courts, apartments. The pilot episode captures the peculiar New York romance of being able to grab a slice of pizza at an all-night place and eating it just out of reach of raindrops. Not that I've ever done that. But isn't it wonderful that I could if I really felt like it?

The chief monkey here is Tom Farrell (Tom Cavanagh), a record-label scout who (unlike Kong) is cursed with an ambivalent heart. Alternately thwarting and torpedoing relationships, he's not an easy character to get in one episode. As played by Cavanagh (*Ed*), he's not overly cute. There's a strain of George Costanza's prickly self-preservation running through his winnowed leanness—and this is intriguing. Then again, the show doesn't always do him favors trying to make him look cool. Cavanagh can project charm and ambition and frustration. But he does not look like a man born to wear a porkpie hat with any confidence or style. He might as well go out with his head under a taxidermied crow. The show has potential, though. This guy won't be climbing any skyscrapers for love—but how high exactly would he go? How low?

★★★

COMEDY/DRAMA

Photo and accompanying article on the 2006 CBS show "Love Monkey," in which Chris co-starred with Tom Cavanagh. The story appeared in a January 2006 issue of "People" magazine.

Chris with cast and crew members on the set of the 2008 Hallmark TV movie "Moonlight and Mistletoe."

Christian with Sarah, Chris's first wife.

Christian with Goose,
Chris's Labrador.

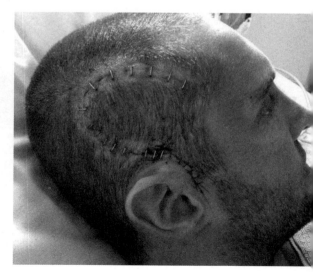

Chris following
his brain surgery
in October 2009.

The lobby poster of "The Devil's Dolls," the horror film
Chris wrote, produced, and starred in, at the Los Angeles
film premiere in September 2016.

Chris, Sharon, Trista, Brett, and Christian at Chris and Sharon's wedding in July 2016.

Chapter 7:
Mostly Sarah

(Oct. 31)

Today is Halloween. My wife Sharon and I are having some folks over to eat chili dogs and help us give out candy to trick-or-treaters, and my stepkids' father is going to take Brett and Trista, Sharon's son and daughter, around our neighborhood to collect their own confectionary bounties. Brett's going as a Los Angeles Rams player, and Trista has a neat old lady getup. My own son Christian is dressing up in an awesome Army Ranger costume I helped him pick out last week.

Only problem is, Christian's going to be trick-or-treating up in Santa Rosa, north of the Bay Area, where he lives with his mother. And it's on days like today that his absence breaks my heart. He was down here in L.A. last year for Halloween, but that's because it was a Saturday; this year, October 31st is on a Monday, so he'd have missed too much school if he'd have come down. It almost physically hurts me to have him living four hundred miles away…but as you'll discover a little later, that's just how things are.

I get up there to see him every chance I get, usually every two or three weekends; he also spends many holidays (and most of the summer) down here with us. What makes that difficult is that it hasn't always been this way; Christian will be eight in a couple of weeks, and for the first five years or so of his life, I was an "every day dad." I was obviously there with him while Sarah and I were together, and even after we split up when he was three, I still saw him every day (and had him every other weekend) until he and Sarah moved up to Santa Rosa. Now, every time I leave him up there to come back home, it tears me up. He always stands on his porch and waves goodbye as I back my rental car down the driveway. He usually cries a little bit, and so do I. And being without him is just…it's as if I'm missing a limb. It's like I come back home with one less arm. I'm not whole.

But in situations like deciding whether or not to have him down for Halloween, as in most situations where Christian is concerned, I've learned from experience to try and look at the big picture. (And of course, the "big picture" is my son and his mental and emotional health.) I try—and I think Sarah does this too—to leave my own feelings out of it. That may mean compartmentalizing some stuff, but in the end, I try to *make decisions that will be the most beneficial to my son.* If I (and/or Sarah) have to suffer some, so be it. But I know for a fact that Christian is the most important thing in my life. In Sarah's, too.

Even at seven years old, Christian is incredibly brave, protective, loyal kid. And despite mine and Sarah's failed marriage, despite all the pain and suffering we caused each other, we've both expressed on numerous occasions that it was all worth it. Because our relatively short marriage, and all the problems that came with it, brought us our beautiful boy. Our Christian. He's named after his Danish great-grandfather. And more than just heritage, his name—"Christian"—is meaningful and perfect. Because every time I see him, or even *think* about him, his very existence reminds me that I need to be a good man.

Sarah and I brought him into the world. And though mine and her relationship ended painfully, it wasn't always bad. No, at first it was full of passion, and playfulness, and love.

At first.

* * * *

"So, what do you do?"

"I'm an engineer."

"Oh, you mean you're one of those people who rides on the backs of trains?"

"No, you idiot. I'm a *civil* engineer."

"Oh. So you figure out how to make people be nice to each other?"

That goofy little exchange, I remember, was part of my first conversation with Sarah, at a bar in downtown Santa Monica back in early 2002. It was in the middle of that brief *First Monday* run, and my buddy Joe Burke and I had walked down to this place called O'Brien's because Joe's girlfriend was having a birthday party there. There were a bunch of women at the party, and Sarah was one of them; she was living in Santa Barbara but had made the two-hour drive over to Santa Monica for her friend's party. We hit it off instantaneously. She was a beautiful girl, but more than that, she was quite different from women I typically dated. I mean, c'mon, she was an engineer! That wasn't even in the same ballpark as the usual entertainment-industry types I went for. After she explained that a civil engineer was somebody who designs and builds roads, bridges, subways, sewer systems—"anything on or below ground," I remember her saying—then I got her number from a friend, and we went on our first date about a week later.

For the first few months, that was how things were: her in Santa Barbara, me in Santa Monica. (She'd moved there after graduating college in Delaware.) I drove over a few times to see her, and it was great. Early on, the thing I liked best about Sarah was that not only was she not involved in the acting business, but she honestly didn't know much about it. And that was incredibly refreshing to me. We *did* both like, however, to go out and enjoy a few adult beverages. And after some drinks, we would get into…well, I think of them as "debates." At least, that's what they were at first. We were different in a lot of ways, and I thought at the time we were just both passionate about our beliefs and had no problem expressing them.

After dating her for about three months, I accompanied Sarah back East to Potomac, Maryland, where she'd grown up, to meet her family. I took an immediate liking to them, and vice versa; I think that trip sort of took our relationship to a new level. So a couple of months after that, she moved down to Santa Monica and in with friends. I was working a ton, mainly on the *CSI* shoots, but I was able to find time for Sarah too. Unfortunately, it wasn't long before our "debates" turned into full-blown arguments. It usually happened after we'd been drinking, and one (or both) of us would say things we'd later regret. We'd always make up within a day or so, but I'm sad to say that that atmosphere of conflict pretty much became the norm.

Cut to the next April when I got *Playmakers*, and I was off to Toronto for seven months. When I told Sarah about it, she said she was happy for me—it was a dream role for me, after all—but I think it concerned her too. I think she felt kind of abandoned, and she wondered whether our relationship would survive such a long separation. For my part, I spent that seven months being totally unsure of what would happen when I got back. I was not yet "all in" where she was concerned. (And I never *would* be all in—you'll see what I mean.)

And sure enough, when I got back to L.A. after *Playmakers* was over, we broke up for a couple of months. Things just came to a head. We fought all the time, we had very little trust in each other, and I know I was drinking too much. Plus, I wasn't ready to get married, and I think she probably was. So we split up for a little bit...and right around that time, *Playmakers* was canceled, and I was in a dark place. Sarah and I tried to work things out; despite our differences, we loved each other (or it felt like we did, anyway). We reconciled after a few weeks, and I quit drinking for about a year. I started going to a twelve-step program, and that *really* helped me evaluate my station in life. And things were a lot better between Sarah and me—for a while.

I did a lot of working and a lot of traveling over the next few months. Among other things, I was in a couple of episodes of a short-lived CBS show called *Clubhouse*, which was based on a book by a former New York Yankees batboy; I also got to go to Hawaii to shoot an episode of *North Shore,* a kind of *Baywatch*-meets-*Dynasty* prime-time soap on which I guest-starred. (I think it was canceled after one season.) Then in the middle of all that, Sarah went on *Wheel of Fortune* with a friend of hers—and they *crushed* it. Won a bunch of cash and a trip to Italy. So we went to Rome, Isle of

Capri, and some other places, and it was awesome. I was sober at the time, remember…and let me tell you: not drinking in Italy is strange. Because *everybody's* drinking, and they don't understand why you're not. To her credit, Sarah cut way down on her own booze consumption, and our "atmosphere of conflict" settled way, way down. It was calm seas between us for the time being.

Toward the end of that year, I got a lead role on *Love Monkey*, a CBS show about a record executive navigating his way through life in NYC. I played Jake, a pro-athlete-turned-sportscaster who was also a closeted gay man, so it was a great, multi-layered character. It also had Tom Cavanagh, Judy Greer, and Jason Priestley; Jason and I became fast friends. I was still sober, and he didn't really understand why…but I told him I planned to not drink for a year, then I'd re-evaluate things. And that year undoubtedly helped me get my head in the right place: I started meditating in the mornings, I was able to concentrate more on my craft, and I started writing screenplays.

We shot the series in NYC—2005, this was—and it was great. We were there for about six months, and that also happened to be the year my beloved Seahawks made their first Super Bowl run. It's funny—I remember I found one bar in Manhattan that showed Seahawks games. At the start of the season, it was on a crappy old TV by the bathroom; by mid-season, when the Seahawks were 7-2, they were on a bigger screen toward the front (and a couple more Seahawks fans started showing up). Then for the last few games, when they were 12-2, 13-2, everybody had jumped on the bandwagon; 'Hawks games were on the bar's main big-screen, and the barstools were lined with customers in Seahawks jerseys. I was like, *hey, where'd you guys all come from?!*

As far as Sarah was concerned: we were both okay with my being in NYC for so long. (That's the impression I had, at least.) We'd both learned a lesson from my *Playmakers*/Toronto absence, and we didn't argue nearly as much this next go-round. When I got back, things were even better between us; absence did, in this case, make our hearts grow fonder. Meanwhile, *Love Monkey*, which was a mid-season replacement on CBS, was pretty much dead on arrival. The network canceled us after only three episodes. (A month or so later, VH1 began airing it and showed eight episodes in all, but yeah. That was the end of that.)

At that point, Sarah and I had been dating for going on four years. And though I've since regretted saying it, I'd already told her that my career was the single most important thing in my life. "If I have to go somewhere for a shoot or something," I'd say, "I *have* to go do it. I love you, but my career comes first." And I realize now that hearing me say things like that couldn't have made her feel very good. Nevertheless, that's where my head (and heart) were. Though I didn't have the capability to be honest, neither with her nor *myself,* about a lot of my true feelings, I was sincere about that, for better or worse.

Now: that said, I cared very deeply about Sarah. I always will. I was thirty-five, and not getting any younger. Sarah had reminded me (both directly and *in*directly) that her biological clock was ticking (she was four years younger than me, so she'd just turned thirty-one when I got back from NYC), and she wanted kids too. And I thought that hey, maybe settling down would be good for me. So, on Memorial Day weekend of that year, I asked her to marry me, and she said yes.

My career, meanwhile, continued its wholly
unpredictable path. I had a role as a recurring character
on CBS's *Jericho*, then the following pilot season was
both great and terrible for me. I was offered the lead
opposite Brooke Shields in an NBC show called *Lipstick
Jungle*. This was in the midst of all our wedding
planning, and I was a happy man—or at least I felt that
way. Then, less than a week before the wedding, I was
fired from the show. "We think you're just too young to
play opposite Brooke," a producer told me. Whatever.
On to the next.

On May 26, Sarah and I got married in Maryland,
and it was beautiful. The reception was at the
Congressional Country Club, a huge, majestic spot in
Bethesda, and the whole affair was like something out of
The Great Gatsby. We honeymooned in Costa Rica,
which was fun—but even then, even in the whole
"honeymoon phase" that is the first few months of
marriage, we just weren't able to sustain much
happiness. There just wasn't much symbiosis to be had.
And pretty much immediately upon our return from
Costa Rica, we started fighting constantly. Within six
months of our wedding, that atmosphere of conflict had

returned—and there it would stay until the end. We started going to counseling, which we would continue off and on until our divorce.

By the beginning of 2008, Sarah and I were basically surviving in a difficult marriage. We were living in a house on 22nd Street in Santa Monica, one that I'd bought and spent several months renovating. We had two dogs, Labradors named Goose and Rowdy, and we paid more attention to our pets than we did to each other. We were seriously like two ships just passing in the night. Even so, Sarah really wanted to have children. It was a strange dichotomy; I myself wasn't sure, but at the same time I wanted to make her happy.

One day in February, I was home sick. I was sitting in the TV room when Sarah came home from work; she sat down next to me on the couch, and after a minute she took a pacifier out of her purse and handed it to me with a huge smile.

I was confused. "C'mon, I'm not *that* much of a baby," I said. "I mean, I'm sick, but I don't feel *that* b —"

"No, dummy," she said. "I'm pregnant."

Chapter 8:
Delivery Rooms and MRIs

(Nov. 9)

It's early November now, and my co-author John and I have been working on this book for about four months. And during that period, more than one person has sort of questioned me about our choice of title. Back when we first decided to call this book *Trying to Walk Like a Man*, I told my mom (who, you may remember, has her Ph.D. in English) about it, and she was confused. "Why is it 'trying' to walk?" she asked. "I've no doubt that you already *do* walk like a man!" Then just last night I was talking to my ex-wife Sarah about the book, and she said pretty much the same thing. So I feel like some clarification is in order.

Listen: life can be difficult. We *all*, every one of us, face struggles. Some more than others. None of us is perfect. And so "*trying* to walk like a man," to me, works on several different levels: for one, it's about physically walking like a mature human being—something I touched on in the introduction—which after my brain surgery, hasn't always been easy. Two, I work in an incredibly difficult business, one in which rejection far outweighs acceptance, so the title is also about keeping my head up—*keeping my forward momentum*—in a profession at which a lot of people simply fail. But more than anything else, it's about *being the best man I can be*. It's about trying to be the best father, the best husband, and the most professional actor/filmmaker that I can. I'm not perfect. I won't always succeed a hundred percent, but I can try. All I can do is the best I can do, as the saying goes.

Today is November 9th. Last night, after the most contentious, divisive campaign of our lifetimes, Donald Trump was elected president. And though I really didn't have a dog in the fight, a lot of people in our country were completely devastated by it. Whether or not he will be a good president remains to be seen. In any case, being a role model for my kids (and for *all* people of younger generations) is as important as ever. If the nation continues to be divided, if society continues bringing hatred and intolerance to the forefront, then teaching young people good morals will become part of the glue that holds us all together. Hopefully, we won't get to that point, but I think it's a good practice anyway.

For Christian, Trista, and Brett, I try to be the best person I can. I try my best to walk like a man, in hopes that they will learn to be good people too. That's what fatherhood is about, isn't it?

Boy. Fatherhood …

* * * *

The memory is crystal clear: after Sarah handed me the pacifier—her way of telling me she was with child—I was over the moon. I remember sort of pacing around with a big shit-eating grin on my face, babbling about who knows what. At some point, I finally sat down on the steps leading into the den to just…breathe. I needed to process the news I'd just been given. And it's interesting where my mind went: rather than considering how I was currently in a troubled marriage, and how having a child would affect our fractured union, Sarah's and my problems became secondary (for the time being, anyway). We were going to be parents. We were overjoyed. That, and *only* that, was on the marital docket at that point. And I know Sarah felt the same way.

So with our spousal issues on the back burner, we commenced with our new roles of parents-to-be. I was working here and there, going on auditions occasionally, but at about month four of Sarah's pregnancy, her doctor said her blood pressure was somewhat high. So she put Sarah on bedrest for the remainder of her pregnancy, which meant I would need to be home with her as much as possible. I had to turn down a few auditions, and had to pass on a couple of actual offers, but I didn't mind. People started excitedly asking us, "Do you want to know whether it's a boy or a girl?!" And that gave me pause. Initially, having a healthy child, regardless of gender, was all that mattered to me. But the more people asked about it, the more I started considering which I'd rather have. And honestly, at the time I thought it might be better to have a girl. (Sorry, Christian, but it's true.) Reason being: I figured I wouldn't be as tough on a girl. Once upon a time, I was a boy, too, so I know more about what it's like. Hence I would probably want to exert more influence on his upbringing, if that makes sense. (And it's funny: I'm much tougher now on Christian and Brett than I am on Trista—but it doesn't matter, because Trista's herself just as tough as the other two.)

So Sarah finally had an ultrasound, and we found out we would have a boy. My previous opinion about the gender didn't matter; I was thrilled. And we realized, honestly enough, that having a boy had always been in the cards. I'll explain: a couple years earlier we'd spent some time with a shaman in Sedona, and at one point he'd said all shamanistically, "I see…I see a little boy here with you." We weren't sure who he meant. One of our fathers? Grandfathers? Immediately after the ultrasound, we knew the shaman was referring to our yet-to-be-conceived son. Whether or not you believe in those kinds of spiritual matters, I'm convinced that Christian's existence, even two years before he came into this world, had already been determined.

Early that summer, I was in the midst of a long jog when his name just came to me. (I get a lot of my best ideas on a run. When I hit mile three or four, and those endorphins kick in and that runner's high floods my brain, the ideas often start flowing like water. More on that a bit later.) Anyway, we were considering names like Porter, Gage, a few others. (And when I told my dad about the "Porter" idea, he immediately said, "Hmm. Is he gonna be carrying everybody's bags?" Good ol' Dad. Suffice it to say that "Porter" was instantly out of the running.) And that day on my run, I thought about my mom's father, Christian, whom I'd been told was a lot like me. (I'd met him when I was really young, but he died when I was six or seven.) He'd owned a shoe store in a small town in Denmark, but everybody said he was also a great entertainer; he'd give toasts and speeches at the drop of a hat, and loved singing, acting, etcetera. We shared that same "hamminess" gene, I guess I'll say. And what better way to honor my grandfather's memory than to name my son after him? When I got home from my run, I told Sarah about it, and she immediately agreed. We decided his middle name would be James, after Sarah's father. So that was it. Christian James. Little C.J.

A couple of months later—in July, I think—we drove up through Cali and Oregon to see my folks in Yakima for a few days. By this point, Sarah and I had become more of a "married couple" than we'd ever been. That may have just been out of simple necessity because of our impending parenthood, but the fact is we were actually getting along. One night while we were in

Yakima, it was pretty hot, so we opened the window before we went to bed. My folks live in a semi-rural part of town, and it's quiet there at night, save for the sound of crickets buzzing away. And I remember that as I was listening to the crickets chirp as I drifted off, I noticed a weird, totally foreign sound mixed in with it: a faint, barely noticeable ringing. I didn't think much of it and went on to sleep, but in the coming days I detected that ringing several more times. I couldn't tell which ear it was coming from, and I again dismissed it as nothing.

In about September, I went to the doctor for my annual checkup, and I mentioned the ringing to him (by that point I noticed it almost constantly). He asked me if I listened to loud music on headphones much, and when I said I did—I played tunes on my iPod when I jogged—he told me that was the likely culprit. "Just turn the music down, you'll be fine," he reassured me. And that was that.

Our son's due date was December 10th, and we were ready. Sarah's parents flew in for Thanksgiving; we had a beautiful meal, then watched the Seahawks get pummeled by the Cowboys in one of the NFL's annual Thanksgiving Day games. We did a bit of Black Friday shopping the next day, then on Saturday, we planned to exchange Christmas gifts with Sarah's folks, since we would have our hands full with a newborn infant on Christmas Day.

At about 7 a.m. that Saturday—November 29, 2008—Sarah's water broke. I drove Sarah and her mom to St. John's Hospital there in Santa Monica, and we got there about 8:00. And at about 11:30, our son, Christian James Wiehl, came into this world. And listen: as anyone who's ever experienced the miracle of childbirth can attest, there is *no other experience that even remotely compares to a child being born.* For me, watching my son's life begin—there are just no words to describe it. My main concern was whether he and Sarah were both okay. And they were. Christian had ten fingers, ten toes…he was eight pounds and eleven ounces of peace, happiness, and love. (I like to joke that he was even polite about being born. The Washington Huskies didn't have a game that day, so Christian was courteous enough to be born on U-Dub's bye week. And since the Seahawks had already played on Thursday, he had the wherewithal to be delivered on a weekend with no football. Haha. Like I said, that's a joke.)

145

Oh, Christian. Our beautiful boy. He and Sarah came home from the hospital a couple of days later, and he was a talisman of goodness and calm from the moment she carried him through the front door of our home. Right away, we noticed how low-key and peaceful Christian was for a newborn; great thing, too, because I think if he'd been fussy or colicky, our house would've literally exploded with everything else that was going on. In the first couple of weeks, Sarah repeatedly complained about the difficulty in breastfeeding Christian, and how low-energy and cheerless she felt in general; we finally realized she was suffering post-partum depression. Sarah's mom had come out to help us for a few weeks, and we were blessed to have here there, but I remember those first few weeks as being extremely tough on all of us.

Meanwhile, the ringing in my ears was getting louder.

I called my doctor and told him that the ringing persisted. "You know, doc," I said, "I think something's wrong. It's getting louder, and I think there may be a problem." He referred me to Dr. Daneshrad, an Ear,

Nose and Throat guy in Santa Monica; I went in and saw Dr. Daneshrad, who gave me a hearing test.

"Huh," he said when the results came back. "You've got a ten percent hearing loss in your right ear." He said it was probably nothing, but he wanted me to get a MRI just to be safe. So I went in and got the MRI two or three days later—December 15th or 16th, this would've been—and I remember calling them to find out the results on the morning of the 22nd or 23rd. The receptionist said that the doctor hadn't had a chance to look at them, and he'd call me back later after he did. But by that afternoon, no call. So I rang them up again, and the receptionist said something a bit odd.

"Um…why don't you just come back in after Christmas? The doctor can explain more then," she said. I thought that was sort of cryptic, but I was like, sure, no problem, and made an appointment for the 26th.

When I got off the phone, Sarah asked me what they'd said. "Oh, they want me to come back in," I told her. "He just wants to talk to me about it. No big deal." I smiled.

Sarah, though, turned white as a ghost. "He wants to explain the test results to you in person? That's not good at all."

Chapter 9:
How I Continued Living

(Nov. 15)

Ever since I was a boy, I've done quite a bit of jogging. (And I know you've heard some of this before, but it bears repeating.) Going on a run is beneficial to me in multiple ways: it keeps me in good physical shape, of course, but it's also when I'm at my most creative. My runs average five or six miles, and about halfway through, the good ol' runner's high kicks in—and over the course of a minute or two, my thoughts become crystal-clear. All the external stuff—my daily schedule, worries about my next audition, etcetera—just goes away. The mechanism is cleared, to put it another way. I get my best ideas then. My son's name, specifics about how to play a particular character, screenplay ideas— those all happen when I'm soaked with sweat, nearly out of breath, and loping along lost in my thoughts.

Speaking of screenplays: Danny Kolker, my *Devil's Dolls* co-writer, and I are currently working on another one. It's a multi-layered, feel-good story about two triathletes. The older one, Chase (the character I'd play),

149

is a former triathlete in his late forties who'd had a stellar career—he'd won numerous Ironman competitions, was the top triathlete in the world, the whole nine. When the story begins, his daughter, in the midst of training for a triathlon herself, tragically drowns; then we jump to ten years later when Chase has basically quit the sport and is just selling cars or something. But then Chase befriends a younger triathlete, who is in danger of having to quit competing because of a developing problem in his shoulder; Chase comes out of retirement to train the kid, and actually decides to start competing again himself. Then…well, I don't want to give it all away, because hopefully, you'll be able to find out for yourself when you see the film at A THEATER NEAR YOU!

Haha. But I honestly believe Danny and I have the makings of what could be a remarkable film. And a lot of the ideas for the story came—you guessed it—when I was on a run. Now that we have the actual story hammered out, we're writing the first act of the screenplay itself. And as you may know, writing for the screen incorporates camera shots into the storyline; the camera-work in a screenplay can be as important as the actual story itself. So these days, while I'm running I sort of "mentally storyboard" scenes; I'm much more creative when I'm struggling through mile five of a jog than I am when I'm just staring at a blinking cursor on my laptop screen. Example: the first scene starts with a shot of Chase's hand on a car steering wheel; he's wearing a wedding ring. The camera pans down, and we see him holding hands with his wife. The next shot is of his kids in the backseat. Then we have an exterior shot of the car passing a sign that says, "IRONMAN COMPETITORS—NEXT RIGHT" or something.

You get the idea. And this mental storyboarding is new for me—but I'm thinking that way because I'd like to direct this one. I'm ready for it. I've considered directing before, but this film will be the first one I've felt familiar and comfortable enough with to give it a go.

I'm excited about this one. It's a feel-good sports picture that's never been done before. And if it gets produced—fingers crossed!—I'll get to do a whole lot more running during filming.

Yeah, there's no doubt that jogging is an important part of my life. But there was a time—not that many years ago, actually—when I thought I might never be able to jog again. Or even walk, for that matter.

* * * *

I'd called my ENT to get the MRI results a couple days before Christmas, and they'd ominously asked me to come back in on the 26th without telling me why. I wasn't worried about it, but the same couldn't be said for Sarah; she was apprehensive as hell. So Christmas that year was pretty surreal. On the one hand, it was our first one with little Christian, who just smiled and took it all in with the expected wonderment of a newborn. But while I wouldn't say we felt a sense of impending doom about the next day's appointment, there was just a feeling of subtle unease that underlaid the whole day.

On the 26th, a friend watched Christian while Sarah accompanied me to Dr. Daneshrad's office. Once there, we were shown into an exam room, and after a few minutes, the doctor came in. Under his arm was a manila envelope that no doubt held the images of my MRI brain scan.

After a bit of precursory small talk, he asked us if we wanted to sit down. I said I preferred standing, but Sarah pulled up a chair. Dr. Daneshrad turned on the light box mounted on the wall—there was a loud *Click!* in the silent room when he flicked the switch—then he took the images out and put three of them, one by one, on the board; the images were views from the right side, left side, and top of my brain. He looked us both over for a moment, his face expressionless.

"The MRI showed an abnormality here, on the right side," he said, tapping the corresponding image. "If you can see this small white spot—that's called an acoustic neuroma." His hand moved to the top-view image, and he pointed to another white dot just to the right of its center. "Here's another view." I heard Sarah gasp from her chair behind me; the doctor continued his explanation. "The good news is that it's benign, meaning—"

"What is it?" I asked. "I mean…what—how—"

"Let me explain," the doctor answered. "It's a small, noncancerous tumor in the area between your inner ear and your brain stem. These things develop over a period of time. Right now it's tiny, about the size of a BB. It won't metastasize—it won't spread to other parts of the body, I mean—but it may grow. How fast, we can't be sure. The problem is, these neuromas develop around three specialized nerves: the balance, the hearing, and the facial nerve. We'll—"

"Then how do we—" I interrupted.

"We'll monitor it closely," he said, holding up a hand to gently interrupt me. "Let me finish, please. We aren't exactly sure what causes these things. It could be stress. It could be radiation exposure—cell phones and such. It could be…anything. Science doesn't tell us much. The good news is, these things are slow-growing. And in my opinion, it looks like we've caught it early. But if it's not removed, it can start to affect your hearing—which in your case, Mr. Wiehl, it's already doing—it can affect your balance, and your facial coordination. If left to grow on its own, it may start to press on your brain stem"—he pointed to the correlating area on one of the images—"and affect basic neurological functions. And eventually, it would be fatal."

I had no words. I looked at Sarah. She was equally wordless, and just stared back at me with wide, tear-brimmed eyes.

"Now: there are basically two types of procedures to remove it," Dr. Daneshrad said. "There's radiation, and there's surgery. Both have their advantages and disadvantages. We don't need to decide anything today." His eyes met mine. "Mr. Wiehl, you're going to be okay. This is not a life-threatening situation. Not yet, anyway. We can take our time deciding the best way to get at this thing."

Sarah, at this point, was fighting back the tears. I went to her and squatted down to look her in the eyes. "I'm going to be okay," I said. "We can do this. *I* can do this." I took her hands and stood up, gently pulling her likewise to her feet. I made arrangements with Dr. Daneshrad for my next appointment, then we left.

Sarah was visibly upset when we went to the car, and for the entire trip home. I was just numb. I remember calling my folks to break the news to them, but I don't recall any details of that conversation. Want to know something weird? The only emotion I remember having was one of gratitude. And by that, I mean I was glad it was me this was happening to. If it had been my one-month-old son, or my wife, or my parents…God, that would've just destroyed me. *But it's me,* I remember thinking. *I can handle this. I* will *do this.*

We got home and continued living.

* * * *

For the next month or so, we just sort of existed. We went about our daily routines like zombies, almost; Sarah was even more depressed, we had little Christian to take care of, and I had to start thinking about finding work in the upcoming pilot season, which was only a few weeks away. Plus, I would soon have to make decisions about my treatment, which would require numerous meetings and doctor visits. The weight of the world was bearing down upon us, that's for sure.

I decided to just take things step by step. First, I set up a meeting in mid-January, if memory serves, at a place called House Clinic to discuss having conventional surgery. I spoke with a Dr. Friedman, a House surgeon, who told me several things about the pros and cons of the surgical procedure. First, he gave me the good news: my tumor was located a relatively good distance away from my facial nerve, so there would be very little chance of any facial damage (palsy, drooping, etcetera); that was good to hear because facial damage would undoubtedly ruin my career. The bad news, he explained, was that the tumor was close to my acoustic nerve, which meant I could possibly lose all hearing in my right ear if the nerve was affected by the surgery. "I'd say you have a sixty percent chance of retaining your hearing," he told me. I thought I could live with that.

Then came the worst news: It was invasive brain surgery, meaning they would have to cut open the right side of my head. And once they did that, they would basically have to sever my balance nerve to get at the tumor. "And I'll be honest: that's not going to be fun," Dr. Friedman said. "When you wake up from the surgery, it's going to be like you're on a spaceship, going backward, underwater. It'll be the most topsy-turvy type of hell you can imagine. You won't be able to focus on anything. And that lasts for several days, until your brain sort of 'reboots' and the balance nerve on the other side recalibrates and takes over." I would be in the Neuro ICU for about three days, and barring any complications, I'd be moved to a private room for the remainder of my recovery. I should be able to go home in about a week.

"We do this type of surgery a lot here at House, and we're very effective. And with this surgery," he finished, "the percentages of fatality are very, very low—one to two percent." I definitely liked those odds. I thanked him and left. At that point, surgery sounded doable. I'd find out more about the radiation, then take it from there.

The next few weeks were extremely tough. Sarah was slow to rise from bed in the morning, so I had to take care of Christian; I was also busy going to/arranging doctor visits. And as the beginning of pilot season neared, I was pretty much at the end of my damn rope. Once I started going on auditions, I knew, there just wouldn't be enough hours in the day to get everything done.

I ruminated on it for a day or two, then I decided that the best thing to do would be for Sarah and Christian to go stay with her parents in Maryland for a few weeks while I tried to book a gig. I needed work to be able to support my family, and I needed time to figure out the best course of action for removal of the tumor. And the most logical way for me to do that, I maintained, was to have a few weeks' time by myself. I could bust my ass trying to get work during pilot season, see more doctors about the tumor issue, then Sarah and Christian could come back home and hopefully, things would be a little clearer.

So I called Sarah's mom and talked to her about it, and she said Sarah and Christian were welcome to come. But when I spoke to Sarah herself about the plan, she was furious. (In retrospect, I can see why.) She was very angry that I went behind her back. She felt like I was abandoning her and Christian. And she didn't want to go in the first place (which is how I knew she'd feel, and the reason I didn't discuss it with her). She finally agreed to make the trip, but she did so very begrudgingly, and she was mad as hell. I don't think she ever forgave me for it.

I didn't talk to her about it beforehand. I own that. And I'm sorry things happened the way they did. But rather than sit here and try to justify my actions, I'll say this: *I made the best decision I could in the situation I faced.* It was a circumstance in which people were going to suffer either way. So I did what I did. I felt like it was the best choice to help us all move forward.

After they had left for Maryland—they planned on being there for three weeks—I got busy. First, I went to Cedars-Sinai Hospital and spoke with specialists there about radiation treatment for the tumor. In a nutshell, this procedure—"radiosurgery," it's called—is *non*-invasive (they wouldn't be cutting my head open, in other words);

159

surgeons use a laser to remove the tumor, with minimal trauma involved. There were two different types of radiosurgery procedures, I learned: CyberKnife and Gamma Knife (which are basically the same; the main differences are that Gamma Knife is done in one session instead of several, and is more specific to cranial procedures). The problem was that radiosurgery was a bit more risky than conventional surgery. They told me that with radiosurgery, there was a fifty- to sixty-percent chance of successfully removing the tumor (as opposed to eighty to ninety percent with a conventional operation). "But if we miss it and hit something else," one of the specialists told me, "we could do permanent damage. And there's a five- to six-percent chance that if we *do* miss the tumor, it will develop into brain cancer. And it would be fatal." Which did *not* sound good. At that point, though I hadn't decided which procedure—conventional surgery or radiation—to choose, I was thinking that cutting my head open was the more appealing option. (Weird as though that may sound.)

In the meantime, pilot season arrived, and I busted said ass looking for work. During the three weeks Sarah and Christian were gone, I must've gone on about fifteen auditions. No jobs in the first week, no jobs in the second week…then BOOM! I got hired—in a big series of commercial spots, oddly enough. I hadn't gone on a commercial audition in years, but I needed to turn over every stone, and I'm glad I did. It was for Ortho products (you know, bug spray, mousetraps and such); I did I think five spots for it, and we filmed them over a period of four days in late February. And it turned out to be very lucrative. Over the next two years or so when the commercials aired, I made several hundred thousand dollars from Ortho. It was an incredible blessing, because I could then concentrate on getting ready— physically, mentally, *and* emotionally—for whatever happened with the tumor removal.

Sarah and Christian came back from Maryland, and the atmosphere in our house was…I guess frigid is the best way to describe it. We totally isolated ourselves from one another, both emotionally and physically. For my part, I began to "gird" myself, if that makes sense, for what was going to be a difficult period. I started building up my defense mechanisms in preparation for my recovery, and part of doing that was making myself less vulnerable, which was not good for my relationship with my spouse. Looking back, I'm sad that it happened that way, but I really didn't have a choice at the time; my survival instinct took over in a lot of ways, and that was how it had to be.

My memory of that summer and early fall is pretty blurred. I didn't work much; I remember doing a car commercial, and I guest-starred on an episode of *CSI: Miami,* and that was about it. I remember spending a lot of time with baby Christian, and drawing a lot of strength and courage from him. In June or July, I think, I decided to have the conventional surgery. For one, the odds of success were better. Like my surgeon said, the recovery would not be fun (and as I found out, "not fun" was putting it extremely lightly!), but I was ready. I was strong—physically, yes, but also mentally and emotionally. And I would need every ounce of my strength.

Later in July, I went up to Yakima to attend my twenty-year high school reunion. Sarah, with her postpartum depression, and I with my impending surgery, were just hanging by emotional threads, really. And it was interesting, because I was the most celebrated graduate of my class, but my life was in complete turmoil. That reunion was a perfect example of the ol' "You can't judge a book by its cover" adage.

I saw my friend again, and she pretty much reiterated what she'd said ten years before: "Well, it looks like you've won this thing." I told her I completely disagreed. Though I didn't mention the tumor or my upcoming surgery, we had a great conversation about the true meaning of success; she was married with kids—and *stable*—and I was…well, "stable" and I weren't even in the same galaxy.

That was how we left it. And as you'll find out later, the tables turned somewhat for her and me—"you can't judge a book by its cover" applied to *both* of us.

Upon my return from Yakima, I worked with my trainers (Thomas Roe, whom I'd been training with for years, and another guy named Tom Williams, a gym owner in Santa Monica) to get in fantastic shape. Outside my immediate circle of family and friends, they were the first people to know about my impending surgery. I eventually told my agents and manager about it, but I didn't give them much of a lead-up because I just didn't want them to worry. I remember going on a couple of trips in August and September: one to Hilton Head, S.C.

for the wedding of one of Sarah's friends, and another to a Washington Huskies game. That U-Dub game was fantastic; it was about three weeks before my surgery, and the Huskies played USC, who were ranked like third in the nation. Even though we'd been 0-12 the year before, we won, and a friend of mine got me on the sidelines for the game. At that point, I was trying really hard not to worry about what was coming, and just live in the moment. And that game was a hell of a moment in which to live.

Then I woke up one Monday morning and realized it was October 12th. My surgery was the next day, at St. Vincent Medical Center in Koreatown. (I would've rather have had it at Cedars-Sinai or somewhere, but St. Vincent is where Dr. Friedman said he preferred to operate, as it was next door to his office at House. And I didn't argue. Home-court advantage, you know?) I also knew I needed to get my head shaved before the surgery. But before I could line up a barber to do it, my trainer Thomas—good ol' T-Roe—said he had some clippers, and he'd do it for free. So I went over to his house, and he shaved my head practically bald. I gave him a hug and

164

told him I'd be back training with him in no time. At least, I hoped I would.

My parents flew in from Washington, so I went to LAX to pick them up. And I had a rule, both for them and for myself: NO TEARS. If one person started crying, we would all bawl. So no tears. I was as upbeat as I could be, and I think my being convivial in spite of what was about to happen was contagious. Everybody was in good spirits (or at least it seemed that way to me).

We went back to my house. Lis was in town, so she was there, and we all sat down for a beautiful dinner; I don't remember exactly what we ate, but I had dietary restrictions before my surgery, so I remember not being able to eat anything heavy.

I remember at one point just looking around the room at my family, and my gaze finally settled on little Christian. He was sitting there contentedly in his high chair, just taking it all in. That made me nearly break my own rule and start sobbing like a little girl. But they wouldn't have been tears of sadness, or fear, or frustration, but tears of gratitude. Because of *him*. *He* was the reason I could survive. *He* was the one who gave me the courage to keep living. *He*…was part of *me*.

Less than twelve hours later, a surgeon was cutting my skull open with a saw, and that courage was a godsend.

Chapter 10:
A Spaceship, Going Backward, Underwater

(Nov. 21)

Last week I got about twenty tattoos.

I got a neat broadsword/skull design on my chest, a cool pair of revolvers on my belly, and two crossed machine guns on my shoulder, along with numerous others with the same "death and violence" theme on my upper arms, back, and forearms. Wicked cool, right?

Yeah, that's what I thought you'd say. Okay, full disclosure: they're not permanent ones. Two special-effects makeup people spent a couple hours applying the "stickers" all over my upper body, then coloring them in with markers, for a guest-starring role I just did. It was for an episode of *NCIS*, and it was a great experience. I got to play an anarchist skinhead-type character (hence all the evil tattoos) who, years before, had stolen a dirty bomb, and the NCIS crew has to track him down. I spent four days on-set; I had a lot of scenes with Mark Harmon, who's one of the kindest, most professional actors I've ever worked with.

And that brings me to my main point: I've long believed that being a guest star on a TV show, particularly one as long-running as *NCIS* (it's in its fourteenth season now), is the most difficult acting job there is. I say that because you're asked to come in with a new character to a show in which the series regulars have had plenty of time to develop their own characters. As a guest star, you have to go in and be one of the leads of that episode, often times with only one or two days of lead-time to work with the script. You have to nail it from the beginning. And not only that, you have to do it in *somebody else's office*. The series regulars are home—they know the crew, each other, and the roles they play. You're a stranger, and you're expected to walk in and crush your part? It's tough, man. And unfortunately, a lot of people on TV series sets can be standoffish, even downright nasty, to outsiders. That's why I've made sure, in my time as a series regular, to bend over backward trying to make guest stars feel welcome.

But I have to say again that my experience on *NCIS* was fantastic. I actually hadn't been sure I wanted the job, as I'm not a huge fan of the show, but when I saw that most of my scenes were with Harmon, I agreed. He has the reputation of being a great guy, fun to work with, and all the rest. So I got the job, and when I went in there, I realized that Mark Harmon's good-guy reputation didn't do him justice. He was welcoming, helpful, generous…I could go on and on. I've worked with some absolutely fantastic people—Joe Mantegna, George Newbern, and Tom Cavanagh come to mind—and Harmon is right up there with the best. Those four days were awesome from beginning to end. Plus, I got some cool tattoos out of the deal.

Yeah. Getting those tattoos was great. It took the two makeup people a couple of hours to apply them: first they put on the stickers, but then a majority of their time was spent coloring them in with markers. While the makeup people worked, I was reminded of another time someone used a marker on my body: October 13, 2009, when a nurse drew a line on my scalp. The line was to show the surgeon exactly where to cut my skull open.

* * * *

Be-beep…be-beep…be-beep…

I remember rolling over and slapping my alarm silent. The digital readout said 4:00 a.m. In my sleep haze, I remember thinking, *Why the hell am I waking up so*...then the realization hit: *Oh yeah. Brain surgery today.*

I showered and dressed; Sarah was up and moving around, as she would go with me to the hospital. She had a granola bar or something, but per doctor's orders I didn't have a bite. We got on the road for the thirty-minute drive to St. Vincent a little before 4:30.

And we actually made it there in great time, because traffic was extremely light (but not deserted; L.A. roads, no matter the time or location, are *always* populated with at least a few vehicles). Sarah and I were pretty quiet during the trip, and the only sound was the omnipresent *whoosh* of the cool pre-dawn air coming through the partially open windows.

We got to the hospital a little before 5:00. I was in good spirits, considering the day's schedule. We went in, filled out some more paperwork (that stuff never ends, does it?), then we went upstairs, and they started to prep me for the surgery at about 6:00. They started two different IVs—what they were for, I have no idea—and performed other miscellaneous preparatory tasks. They also marked an area on my abdomen from which the surgeons would take fat; they would use the abdominal fatty tissue to "patch" the skull incision.

But I'll tell you: when a nurse started marking my scalp with a felt tip pen to delineate where the surgeon should cut my skull—*that* was when it became real. I was about to have my head cut open. I'd be lying if I said I didn't feel a little fear at that point. But honestly? What I felt more than anything else was a sense of calm. The mechanism was clear. I could do this. And I was again thankful that it was happening to me instead of anyone else I loved.

Then, with all the prepwork done…we waited. Sarah was there with me, and I remember telling her that I loved her, I loved Christian, and if anything were to happen to me, to just keep going. I'd actually prepared a will not long after my diagnosis…just in case.

Just in case.

At about 8:30, I said goodbye to Sarah, and they wheeled me up to the OR. I went into another sort of prep room, where I met the operating team, headed by Doctors Friedman and Schwartz. There was also a surgical nurse whose sole responsibility was to watch the video monitor to make sure the neurosurgeon stayed away from my facial nerve. (If he accidentally nicked it or something, the results would be disastrous. Among other things, my career would be over.)

And then it was time.

As they wheeled me into the OR, two things instantly struck me: it was friggin' *cold*, and it was friggin' *small*. I've since found out that medical staffs prefer ORs to be cold; since the human body temperature rises in stressful situations, surgeons feel most comfortable in an OR that's about 60 degrees. And as for the size of the room: I was expecting a larger, more dramatic "operating theater"-type situation. I've been in ORs, but they were TV show sets like *ER* and *Private Practice*, and those were huge. (Of course, they had to be, to have room for the cameras and sound equipment and stuff.) But this room was small, a bit dark, and sterile (obviously). There just wasn't much to it. It was pretty anti-climactic, I'll say.

At that point it was just me and the anesthesiologist in the room, as everybody else must've been scrubbing up and whatnot. I remember trying to make jokes, i.e., "I played a doctor on TV, so if anybody needs help, I can take over"…that sort of thing.

Then, after a couple of minutes, he simply said, "Okay. Here we go." I saw out of the corner of my eye that he was fiddling with one of my IVs. Then he turned to me. "I'd like you to count backward from ten."

"Okay. Ten, ni…"

Fade to black.

* * * *

The surgery lasted for seven hours. Obviously, I wasn't awake for it. But I've had extensive conversations with my folks since then to find out exactly what they did during that time.

My parents had arrived at the hospital shortly before my surgery began at 9:00, and they were shown into a waiting room just down the hall from the OR. The waiting room was right next to the post-surgical recovery room, where I'd be taken when—*when*, not if!—I made it through the craniectomy. Mom said they sat restlessly in the waiting area for only a few minutes, then they both explored the hospital's halls. They were both pretty anxious, and they didn't notice much during their rambling. They met up for a tasteless lunch of hospital food in the cafeteria at noon, then continued their uneasy exploration. Dad roamed through seemingly every hallway of the hospital's seven floors, and eventually returned to the fourth-floor OR waiting room. Mom soon joined him.

And they waited.

And waited.

And waited.

Mom said those seven hours were gruesome, but she tried to focus on my strength. And not just my physical power, but on the resilience of my spirit. The power of my *soul* was what kept her going.

Their souls, meanwhile, were fraught with unease. Neither of them could keep from glancing at the clock on the wall every five minutes or so. They read every magazine on the table. They used the restroom. They drank coffee, then used the restroom again. They talked, they shifted in their seats, and they waited.

And they waited.

Though Mom knew doing so was pretty grim, as the hours wore on she couldn't help thinking about me through the years; it was almost as if while my head was cut open, my life flashed before *her* eyes, if that makes sense.

Halloween of '78 when I was seven, when I dressed as Chewbacca.

Early 1981, and me struggling through the snow on that Mount Rainier hike when I was ten.

My senior portrait from '88, and how much my budding good looks had reminded her of Dad.

How proud she'd been when she saw the Lee Jeans commercial in 1995—my first paid acting gig.

She said she finally had to pick up a magazine to keep from bursting into tears.

So they waited.

Then, at a couple of minutes after 3:00—Mom said she remembered the time because she'd just looked at the clock, of course—their wait was over. Dr. Friedman, the ENT who'd been the lead surgeon, came through the door to the waiting room, his surgical mask hanging from his neck and a smile on his face.

"Okay, we're done," he said. They were able to get the tumor successfully, and there was no damage to my facial nerve. "But it's too early to tell about the auditory nerve," he said. "We'll just have to wait and see." The worst thing, he went on, was that because the surgery required severing my balance nerve to reach the tumor, my sense of equilibrium would be non-existent for up to forty-eight hours. "Christopher will have no sense of direction, and that will make him very nauseated. I just want to give you fair warning."

Mom said that yes, I'd told them all about it. (My guess is, I probably told them even more than they wanted to know.)

"Okay then," Dr. Friedman said. "Let's go see him."

Though my memories of that time are unbelievably jumbled, I think I was just starting to regain consciousness when they came into the room. In a way, I sort of recall it in third-person, as if I were witnessing some poor soul waking up from surgery. But—no, it happened to me. I remember how confusing and surreal those first few minutes were, no doubt. Maybe this was my brain going into survival mode here, but the best way I can express that frightening period is in script form.

FADE IN:

INT. SURGICAL RECOVERY ROOM - DAY

CHRISTOPHER is lying in a hospital bed, eyes closed; the top of his head and his right ear are covered with gauze. IV tubing runs from his left arm to a solution bag. The bed is surrounded by various medical machinery — a heart monitor, the IV stand, etcetera. The room is silent except for the ever-present BEEP…BEEP of the heart monitor.

SARAH is standing to the left of the bed. One by one, INGA, DICK, and LIS join her at CHRISTOPHER's bedside. After a moment, INGA leans over to kiss her son's forehead. CHRISTOPHER's eyes flutter momentarily, but remain closed.

No one speaks. After a few seconds, DR. FRIEDMAN joins the others at his bedside.

177

DR. FRIEDMAN

And...here's our boy. Has he shown any
signs that he's waking up?

DR. FRIEDMAN leans down to his patient.
CHRISTOPHER's eyes flutter again, and he
MOANS softly.

INT. RECOVERY ROOM - CHRISTOPHER'S
P.O.V.

A slow, erratic FADE IN on DR.
FRIEDMAN'S face, with the ceiling in the
background—only there are three faces, not
one, and all three are drifting fluidly
around the frame. Slow FADE OUT, then
another FADE IN on the doctor's face; it's
now doubled, upside down, and drifting
sideways. We see the doctor smile broadly;
suddenly there are numerous faces, as if we
are seeing them through a kaleidoscope.
Then back to three, then two, then a single
face; the images remain blurry yet fluid,

and constantly in motion, like swiftly
drifting clouds.

    DR. FRIEDMAN
    his face now tripled)
    Welcome back. How are you feeling?

    CHRISTOPHER
    laughing)
    Is that all ya got? Let's do it again!

We hear the others LAUGH loudly, almost
in desperation. The light FADES, then
BRIGHTENS, with DR. FRIEDMAN's face
continuing its drifting, multiplying dance.

    DR. FRIEDMAN
    Honestly though, Chris—how are you
doing? Okay?

    CHRISTOPHER
    Like ten miles of bad road, doc. Ten
miles…

DR. FRIEDMAN

I bet. Well, like we talked about, you're going to be pretty unsettled for a while. Just bear with it. The good news is that your procedure was a success. I'm pretty sure we got most of the tumor. We'll know for sure when—

CHRISTOPHER

My hearing?

DR. FRIEDMAN

Pardon?

CHRISTOPHER

My hearing. Were you able to save it?

At that, we see DR. FRIEDMAN's numerous, floating faces cloud for an instant.

DR. FRIEDMAN

Well…we're just not sure yet. Here, let's give it a try.

The doctor's hand comes rushing past the frame, trailing flesh-colored streams of light behind it. The dazzling white of his sleeve swirls and fills the screen.

DR. FRIEDMAN (cont.)
Can you hear this?

We hear CLICK, CLICK as the doctor snaps his fingers next to CHRISTOPHER's right ear.

CHRISTOPHER
I…maybe? I…not sure. I don't know…

DR. FRIEDMAN's face zoooooooms to the right and out of the frame. We see the fiberglass ceiling tiles dance, fade in and out, and multiply all at once. The image is blurry, then suddenly sharp, suddenly upside down, then multiplied, and drifting all the while.

181

DR. FRIEDMAN (O.S.)

It's too early to know for sure. We'll be able to test it in a few weeks. But…

DR. FRIEDMAN's voice fades. Meanwhile, the ceiling tiles are kaleidoscoped, swimming, and leaning crazily in every direction. Then they start spinning.

CHRISTOPHER

Dad. Hey Dad!

DICK's spinning, multiplied face zooms into the frame.

DICK

I'm here.

CHRISTOPHER

Get everybody out. Gonna be sick. Everybody *out.*

INT. RECOVERY ROOM - DAY

DICK herds everyone out of the room as CHRISTOPHER vomits all over his neck and chest. Nurses rush over to assist, but there is little they can do as he continues vomiting.

* * * *

I stayed in the OR recovery room for several more hours; I couldn't be moved up to the Neuro ICU until the surgical anesthesia completely wore off. A few folks came to see me, and though my world was turned upside down (both literally and figuratively), I was actually able to talk to them a little bit. Mostly, though, I just slept.

At about 8:00 p.m., a team of nurses wheeled me up to the Neuro ICU on the seventh floor. Though my memory is pretty hazy, I think there were only four beds in that unit. And Dr. Friedman's "spaceship" analogy applied here too: it was dark, it only had the most vital equipment, and everybody talked really softly. The patients in there were recalibrating their brains, so I think the hospital wanted us to have as little mental stimuli as possible.

I spent the next three days in the relative belly of the Neuro ICU spaceship. Sarah, my folks, and a few random friends visited me (but only for brief periods, and usually one at the time, as visitation in the unit was extremely limited). Nurses gave me intermittent sponge baths, whispering greetings to me while they worked. Every few hours, Dr. Schwartz—the neurologist in charge of my post-surgical care—would check on me; he would gently peel back the gauze covering the seven-inch long suture running along the right side of my head to make sure the staples were in place and the suture wasn't leaking. I slept ninety percent of the time—until Friday morning, when they moved me to a private room in Neuro Recovery.

* * * *

Drip.

A couple of hours after my move, Sarah was sitting in my new place of accommodation, leafing through a magazine while I dozed. Mom and Dad were off grabbing lunch, and were to return to my room after the meal.

Drip.

About once a minute, Sarah told me later, clear fluid was dripping from my nose onto my hospital gown. After a few minutes, Sarah said something. "Babe. Your nose is running?" Sarah gave me a Kleenex from the nightstand, and I used it to wipe my nostrils. "Don't you think we should let them know?"

"C'mon," I said. "A *runny nose*? What's the big deal? I'm okay, I promise."

"Well…" Sarah had a worrisome frown on her face (a look which, unfortunately, I'd come to know all too well). "I think we need to tell a nurse. Seriously. I th—"

"It's a runny nose! What's the—I'm fine."

But Sarah held firm. "Chris: either you tell them, or I will."

I remember feeling exasperated—and tired as ever. "Fine. Go tell 'em."

She was gone for several minutes, and returned with a resident whose nametag read "Deon." His coal-colored skin offset a wide grin full of teeth.

"Mr. Wiehl, I hear you got tissue issues," Deon said with a huge smile. "You feeling okay?"

"Well, under the circumstances...sure! Never felt better!" We both laughed.

"Okay. I'd like you lean forward, and..." He withdrew another tissue and spread it across my lap. "Hold your head over this."

"Um, okay." I held my head as he directed. For a few seconds ... nothing. Then:

Plop.

Plop, plop.

Several drops of mucus dripped onto the tissue. "Okay," Deon said, and handed me another Kleenex. "You can clean up." I wiped my nose, as blowing it was strictly forbidden at that point.

"Is...is there a problem?" The question was from Sarah.

Deon flashed his dazzling smile. "Aw, nothing to worry about, ma'am. Dr. Schwartz will explain it. He'll be by in a little while." And with that, he left.

Sarah's worry frown remained. "I don't like this," she said.

"It's nothing," I said. "You heard the guy."

186

But my runny nose turned out to be quite something indeed.

* * * *

Dr. Schwartz came by a few minutes after Deon's visit; he performed a thorough exam of my nasal passage (including the collection of a sample of the clear discharge within it), along with another detailed inspection of my cranial suture. He was quiet the whole time. "I'll be back in a couple of minutes," he said as he left the room, and he took the sample with him, I assumed to test it. When he came back he spoke very matter-of-factly to the four of us (me, Sarah, and my folks, who'd arrived while Dr. Schwartz was gone).

"The fluid sample from your nose tested positive for beta-2 transferrin, which means it is not mucus. Beta-2 transferrin is a glycoprotein that's found exclusively in cerebrospinal fluid. Unfortunately," he told us, "it seems like the patch isn't holding up. The cerebrospinal fluid—CSF, we call it—is leaking from the skull suture into your nasal cavity." He paused and looked around. "The issue can be treated several different ways, one of which is surgery to mend the leak. But I don't think that's necessary. No matter what procedure we choose, we need to perform it right away. Because if left untreated, the level of fluid in the cavity surrounding your brain will drop, which can cause infection and brain swelling.

"And it will be fatal."

I remember hearing Mom and Sarah gasp involuntarily at that, but I tried to focus on Dr. Schwartz's eyes (and with my vision still pretty screwy, it was hard). And oddly enough, what my *mind's* eye saw was not the doc, but an image of my little Christian, just sitting in his high chair. That gave me more strength than I knew I even had. I decided to keep fighting. To make it home so I could hold my son in my arms. To *beat* this goddamn thing.

"Then Doc," I said, "tell me what we need to do."

* * * *

Since I was still heavily medicated, my memories of the next few hours are pretty blurry. But apparently Dr. Schwarz decided to put in a lumbar drain to regulate the amount of CSF, and to slow (and hopefully stop) the nasal leak. And inserting the drain in my lumbar vertebrae, unfortunately, required a good ol' spinal tap; though I was drifting in and out of consciousness throughout the day, I was required to remain awake while a nurse injected a long, thick needle into the base of my spine, through which the drain tube was inserted. And as anybody who's had one can attest, spinal taps aren't much fun. Though the nurse gave me a local anesthetic to numb my lower back, the feel—the *pressure*—of the needle traveling along my spinal cord was enough to make me grit my teeth and growl.

Let me get all technical for a second: the critical factor in using a lumbar drain was monitoring the level of CSF collected. Too much fluid, the brain would dry out and swell; too little fluid, the nasal leak would continue. So to aid in this CSF drain monitoring, Dr. Schwartz, who had dealt with the issue before, had recently devised a specialized device: an apparatus that, in a nutshell, used a basic carpenter's level to constantly gauge the level of drainage. If the drain container got too full, meaning too much CSF was being collected, the level would tilt one way, and vice versa. Dr. Schwartz had only just begun using the level device on patients, but he had trained all the Neuro Recovery nurses on how to configure and use it. After Dr. Schwartz made sure my device was working properly, he apparently left.

And that was when things got dicey. First, the hospital staff decided that I could not stay in my room in Neuro Recovery. The CSF monitoring device would need to be checked regularly, and since the Neuro Recovery Unit reduced its staff on Saturdays and Sundays, it didn't have the available manpower to properly monitor the fluid levels over the weekend. I also couldn't be moved back to the Neuro ICU, as that unit apparently didn't admit patients on Fridays.

So for some reason, they concluded that the best spot for me was in the general ICU on the first floor, which had nurses twenty-four hours a day, and they'd be able to keep an eye on Dr. Schwartz's ingenious device.

The problem: the general ICU nurses had no idea how to do it.

At 7:00 or 8:00 that evening, I woke from a doze, and I was startled when I saw my new surroundings. My brain was still pretty damn fuzzy, so I could recall only bits and pieces of the day's events: the weird, foreign pressure in my back during the spinal tap…the elevator sinking down, down as I was being transferred to the first floor…Dr. Schwartz explaining to an Asian woman (a nurse?) how to monitor the fluid levels, and the woman not seeming to understand a thing he said…Mom kissing my cheek and telling me they'd see me in the morning. I remember glancing around at the quiet hustle-and-bustle of the ICU and discovering I felt very alone. And very uneasy.

At one point, I remember, I closed my eyes to try and still my mind; after only a few moments, though, I heard voices to my left and opened them again. The Asian nurse (and she was indeed a nurse, I'd determined, as I'd seen her tending to other patients) was standing with another female nurse, this one undoubtedly Hispanic. They were in a two-person huddle next to my CSF fluid drain, and the Asian nurse was trying to explain—in extremely broken English—how the leveling apparatus worked. As the conversation haltingly progressed, the Hispanic nurse answering in equally broken monosyllables, I grew increasingly dismayed. *They have no fucking clue how that thing works,* I thought. *I'm going to die.*

I closed my eyes again and tried to relax. The nurses continued their painfully confusing conference.

When I opened them once more, my vision swam again…and when it finally settled, I was looking at the wall across the room.

On the wall was a small, unassuming crucifix, less than a foot in length.

I stared at the cross for a few seconds—and I was transformed. I've never been a religious man, but the sight of that crucifix, and the nearly inconceivable power it represented, flooded me with spiritual strength. I truly believe a minor miracle occurred at that moment. My mind retrieved the image of my son smiling up at me from his high chair…and that was all it took.

I'm not going to die today.

"Excuse me," I said to the two nurses, scooching up in my bed. When they didn't respond, I repeated my request—only this time it was more of a command.

"*Excuse* me!" The nurses jumped and stared at me, startled. "I need you to bring me a phone."

Chapter 11:
I Get By With a Little Help from My Friends

(Dec. 1)

Today is the first day of December. Last week, Sharon and I hosted Thanksgiving for the first time as a married couple, and it was absolutely splendid. My folks, Sharon's mom Jan, and Christian all joined me, Sharon, Brett, and Trista for the holiday, and we had a marvelous time. We ate a fantastic meal, of course, but that was just a small part of it.

First, Thanksgiving morning most of us participated in the Pacific Palisades Turkey Trot, an annual 5K charity run here in our neighborhood. (It wasn't my first time to run in it, as I'd—well, we'll get to that.) I ran with Christian and Brett, and they completed the race in pretty good time; then I went back and finished with seven-year-old Trista. They all walked a little bit here and there, but I made sure they had strong finishing kicks. Plus, my mom and dad—both eighty—walked it and finished it too. It was great to work with the kids on athletic concepts: pacing, finishing strong, and learning to work through pain. Those are lessons I learned running track when I myself was young, and I've put them to great use as an adult, so it was unbelievably satisfying to pass them on.

Then we had the obligatory Thanksgiving feast, and like I said, it was great—but Black Friday was even better. Not a single one of us went shopping. Instead, my dad, my son and I watched the annual Apple Cup, which is the name of the University of Washington-Washington State game. As you can imagine, it's the biggest college game of the year in the state of Washington (as all in-state rivalry games are in their respective areas). This year's game was especially good, as U-Dub was ranked fifth in the nation going in, and Wazuu was #23. So three generations of us Wiehls sat down to watch two great teams battle it out.

And my Huskies whooped 'em 45-17. Afterward, I got to enjoy another tradition: one of my oldest friends Brian King—we've been buddies since the first grade—is a lifelong Washington State fan. So he and I have a deal: whoever's team wins each year, that person calls the other after the game—and the loser *has* to pick up the phone and take his medicine. We've been doing that for years, and it's always a chance for some good-natured ribbing combined with some catching up on each other's lives. It's an annual ritual that I've come to cherish.

And after the game, Christian, Brett, Trista and I got down to business—both literally and figuratively—with another Wiehl family tradition:

Monopoly.

It was a fantastic time. I *so* loved watching them learn how to make deals on properties, and start to understand sportsmanship. Invariably, one of them would get upset if the game wasn't going their way—but we had a rule: no crying. (Because, hey: There's No Crying in Monopoly!) And since I'm the undisputed Monopoly KING…I crushed them to smithereens. Though you may laugh, I honestly think that learning to lose gracefully is an important life lesson. (Goodness knows, I've had to learn the hard way!)

The whole Thanksgiving holiday was special because I got to be a dad, a friend, and a part of the family. And it was a time I'll never forget. My love for family and friends has been an integral part of my life since…well, forever. And metaphorically speaking, that love has even kept me alive.

* * * *

It was do or die—literally. And I mean *literally* do something, or literally cease living.

That Friday evening in the general ICU, when I realized the nurses had no idea how to operate the mechanism that was keeping me alive, I knew I had to act. The mere thought of my family coming back to the hospital to see me in the morgue, or my son having to grow up without his father, was more than enough to propel me into action. Even though my balance was still pretty shot, and I was heavily medicated (and thus drifting in and out of reality), I knew I had some work to do. Enough fucking around.

I demanded a phone, and the nurses finally dragged out a stool with the red, rotary-dial ICU desk phone atop it, the long gray cord still attached. Though I'm pretty sure I still remembered how to use a rotary dial (haha), my vision was still swimming too much to properly focus on the phone, so I had a nurse dial my home number for me. Sarah answered—she and my folks had just gotten home, and were sitting down to dinner—and I said something to the effect of, "Somebody needs to get down here now, or they're gonna kill me." So she and Dad jumped right back in the car. But since our house was in Santa Monica, it would take them a while to get there, so Sarah called her good friend Danielle, who lived on Fairfax Avenue (less than a ten-minute drive from St. Vincent) and asked if she could go immediately.

Danielle and her husband Scott arrived about thirty minutes later. By that point, I was raising absolute hell with the ICU staff. I told them stuff like: "Listen, you need to get your shit in a sock here. You have somebody who doesn't know what the hell she's doing, trying to explain to somebody else what to do? Get Dr. Schwartz on the phone *immediately* and find out how this thing works, or some heads are gonna fuckin' roll." (Excuse the outburst, but I'm trying to recall it like it actually happened. I mean, I was pissed. I *was* trying to stay alive and all.)

For better or worse, my assholishness worked. By the time my dad and Sarah got there at 9:00 or so, the nurses were trying to track down Dr. Schwartz. Meantime, it was decided that for the remainder of my time in the hospital (or at least until I got out of the ICU), somebody would stay with me at all times. I needed an advocate. St. Vincent was a downtown hospital, and the ICU just wasn't as high-caliber as some others in the city. I mean, gunshot victims were much more the norm than neurosurgery patients, you know? So it would be to my advantage to have somebody on my side—somebody *there* with me.

My dad stayed with me that night. And the medical staff eventually got hold of Dr. Schwartz, who gave them step-by-step instructions on how to use the level-drain apparatus. And after they learned what to do, the nurses were fantastic.

I was in that ICU for another five days. My family and friends stayed with me in shifts—usually one or two during the day, then one each night. I remember that Mom stayed with me a couple of times, and she and I engaged in an activity that we hadn't done for…shoot, thirty years, at least. It was an incredibly useful way to pass the time, and it was also meaningful, almost profound:

She read to me.

She started with some popular novel she'd picked up from the hospital gift shop or somewhere, by somebody like James Patterson, but we quickly agreed the book was completely unfulfilling. But then she read from one of her own books, by a German-American author named Ursula Hegi (who's actually one of Mom's contemporaries, as she was a literature professor for years at Eastern Washington University), and that was infinitely better. It was one of her earlier books: *Stones*…shoot. *Stones from the*…something. Oh yeah: *Stones from the River.* I don't remember the book's specific subject, but given the situation, I remember it bringing me a lot of comfort. Mom reading to me in her slight Danish accent amidst the madness of the downtown L.A. ICU brought some much-needed peace to an otherwise stressful environment.

So the days crept by. Some friends came by from time to time, including my buddies Phil and Kathy…funny story about that. Phil's a great guy: he's 6'7", was on that show *American Gladiators* for a year or two, and an interesting about him is that he runs on "Phil time." (Meaning he's always late. *Always.*) Anyway, he volunteered to stay with me one night, said he'd stop by and grab me an In N' Out Burger on the way, yada yada. (And if you've never had the luxury of eating one of those magical burgers, you have not lived, my friend.) So, of course, he shows up at the hospital like two hours late. "I couldn't find it," he said when he arrived. The burger was ice-cold (but don't think for a *second* I didn't still eat that bad boy). And the main reason for his being there was to stay up (at least until I went to sleep) and make sure everything went smoothly. So what does Phil do? Not thirty minutes after he got there, he fell asleep in a chair. (Which was fine, as the night was uneventful, but it's still funny.)

Listen: by no means am I criticizing Phil. On the contrary, I'm incredibly indebted to him. Because even though he was late, he showed up. He was there for me. That's what friends do—they *show up.* I consider myself *so*, so fortunate that a lot of people supported me in my time of need. Shoot. My heart is swelling now just thinking about it. People are beautiful sometimes, you know?

Ahem. Where was I? Oh yeah—the ICU. When you think about it, the human body is such a miraculous thing, isn't it? I was at a point where I could've died. Fortunately, I didn't. And right away, my body (and in particular, my *brain*) started healing itself. Sure, I had medical assistance, but by about the third day in the ICU,

I could feel myself starting to make a comeback. Once the fight-or-flight, "panic mode" feelings went away, and I was sure I was going to live, I began to sort of take stock. My biggest concern was whether or not I'd lost my hearing in my right ear. My head was still wrapped, so I wasn't able to really test it, and therefore unsure; even so, I remember that as the days passed and I got stronger (and less dizzy!), the biggest feeling I had was one of gratitude. I was in a big-city ICU, remember, and there were people coming in with all sorts of horrible injuries. Several people died while I was in there, and while I was sad for them, I was incredibly grateful it wasn't me. There but for the grace, you know?

After five days, thank *God*, the CSF leak had stopped, so they moved me back up to Neuro Recovery. I already felt like I wanted to get the hell out of there, but the unofficial test for me being recovered enough to leave was being able to make it to the bathroom on my own—and that short walk to the potty, even though it was only a few feet, was still several days away. When I first moved back to that unit, I could barely stand up, let alone walk. Even so, I tried that first day to make it the pisser, and failed miserably; I fell, and had to be helped back into bed.

But being back in a private room was relative heaven. For one thing, it was tons more peaceful, which allowed me to relax and focus on getting better. I had a few more visitors, and around that time my sister Lis made something really cool happen: she was back on the air at Fox News, and at the end of an episode of *The O'Reilly Factor*, ol' Bill O'Reilly himself sent me well-wishes and thanked my surgical team for saving my life. It was very touching—especially coming from a self-described curmudgeon like him.

By the third day in there, I felt like a caged animal—which was weird and frustrating, because I couldn't very well do any restless pacing. Regardless, I was *determined* to make it to the bathroom. So early that afternoon, I sat up, swung my legs over the edge of the bed, and slowly—ever so slowly—rose to a standing position. My vision field was still swimming crazily, but the effect was somewhat less than it had been; I summoned all the strength I had to take slow, shuffling steps to the toilet. I did my business, then started back to bed. But: instead of turning right to go toward the bed, I turned left and went out into the hall. "No, this way," the nurse beckoned behind me, but I ignored her. I wanted to prove to them (and to myself, honestly) that I could *walk*, dammit. And I did. I only went partway up the hall and back, but I…fucking…*walked.* I tumbled back into the bed, drenched in sweat and sapped of strength, but I made it.

And within a couple of hours, I went home.

I remember my doctor telling me that "being on the outside," haha, would be difficult at first. The natural light, the movement, etcetera, would play hell on my still-reconfiguring brain. And he was right: when they pushed my wheelchair out the front door, I was like Manfred Mann: blinded by the light, baby. When the car started moving, I got carsick immediately. And when we jumped on the freeway to head back to Santa Monica, it was just crazy, like we were in a fighter jet going Mach 2 or something. It wasn't long before I had to put my hands over my eyes to stop the dizziness. Despite all that, I was incredibly glad to be out of the hospital. I'd been there for eleven days—and that was about ten days too long.

When we got home, my dad helped me out of the car and up the driveway. When I got through the door, the first thing I saw was ten-month-old Christian taking a nap in his crib. He woke up when I came in, and stood up in his crib and grinned at me. And at that moment, all the hell I'd just been through, all the pain, the frustration, the uncertainty…it was instantly erased.

I went over to him. Though I couldn't pick him up (per doctor's orders, I couldn't lift anything heavier than a couple of pounds for a month or two), Sarah held him while I pressed my body against theirs. It was a beautiful moment. I cried. So did everybody else. I remember going to lie down in my bed—my *own* bed—for a few minutes, and my two Labs Goose and Rowdy came and joined me. We had this big bay window in the bedroom; the window perfectly framed a big Chinese elm tree in the yard. And I remember lying there petting my dogs and looking at this tree, and I was nearly overwhelmed with gratitude. I was alive. I was getting better. And I was home.

A little later, we had dinner. I was able to sit at the dining room table with Sarah, Christian, my folks, and Sarah's mom Debbie (who was a nurse, and had flown out to give us a hand for a few weeks). I couldn't sit there for very long (and by "not long," I mean two minutes), but that dinner was unbelievably special. I was *home*.

Sleeping in my own bed that night was absolute heaven.

Chapter 12:
A New Normal

(Dec. 6)

"Get up off the mat."

As you probably know, that's a saying that means to recover from a setback and keep trying. It's a reference to boxing, i.e. when a fighter "gets up off the mat" to continue the match after he's knocked down.

For a good year or so after my brain surgery, getting up off the mat was basically my world—not only figuratively, but literally too. As an athletic guy, I wanted to return to good physical shape as quickly as possible and resume my daily exercise regimen. And I've been able to get back to that level of activity, thank goodness. These days I perform some kind of physical activity six or seven days a week (I sometimes—but not always—take Sunday off). And there are two types of exercise I do that are directly related to "getting up off the mat": boxing and yoga.

I don't actually compete in boxing matches, so I don't literally get off the mat when I box. (I "performed" in boxing matches during filming for *Pensacola: Wings of Gold*, as my character boxed in a match, but that was obviously make-believe.) But about once a week, I work with Thomas Roe, my longtime trainer, on various boxing training techniques: punching the heavy bag and the speedbag, and combinations with a partner who wears mitts. Boxing is about so much more than brute strength, too; it's about speed, coordination, and balance as much as it is power. And these boxing drills were some of the first regular exercise I performed after my surgery. T-Roe had me in the gym doing footwork and mittwork pretty much as soon as I was able to stand; it was good exercise, he said, for my body *and* my brain to have to concentrate on using my feet, my balance, and my coordination when delivering punch combinations. It was an unbelievable help during my early rehabilitation, and it's something I do even now. (I'm actually meeting T-Roe for boxing drills early tomorrow morning, matter of fact.)

Then at the other end of the exercise spectrum, there's yoga (which *is* literally getting up off the mat— the yoga mat). I started doing it years ago at a place called YAS (which stands for "yoga and spinning") down in Venice, under the tutelage of the incredible

Kimberly Fowler. Yoga, as you probably already know, helps strengthen your core, it increases your balance and flexibility, and best of all, it helps quiet your mind. As an actor, I benefit greatly from all these things. And during my rehabilitation, the "becoming one with mind and body" has been invaluable, as the surgery had really sort of disconnected the two. Now I go to a place called YogaHop in Brentwood; it's a ninety-minute workout, and I come out of there drenched in sweat but incredibly relaxed and focused.

Indeed, I'm truly blessed to again be able to work out every day. Since I'm forty-six, I vary the types of workouts I do, too: in addition to the aforementioned boxing and yoga, I jog, bicycle, do calisthenics, and now I even swim at the Palisades High School pool. (The swimming took a while after my surgery because of my balance issues, but I'm glad to be doing it again.) And then on Saturday morning, the sort of culmination of all my workouts is a class with Tom Williams, my other trainer, at Burn Fitness in Santa Monica. It's an eighty-minute cross-training session, and it's 4,800 seconds of pure hell—and I love it. I mean, we get *after* it. Tom mixes it up with all sorts of calisthenics, stair work, sprints, ropes…we move the entire time. I've been doing that class for eight years now—I started a year or so before my surgery—and the other class members and I are like a family. One of my ultimate goals after the surgery was to get back to participating in Tom's Saturday class; I actually started going back three or four months after I got out of the hospital. At first I could only go for a few minutes at a time, but I slowly increased my endurance, and now I can do the whole eighty minutes again.

As I said, it's a blessing to be able to work out like I do. But as you'll see, at one point for me, a "workout" consisted of walking to the end of the driveway.

* * * *

I was going to go trick-or-treating, dammit. I *was*.

Sure, that sounds like a complaint a seven-year-old would make, but for me, it was a huge deal. I got home from the hospital in late October, with Halloween about a week away. And right away I began focusing on getting better. Getting my strength back. So I started setting daily goals: the first day, I would walk to the front door by myself. "That's what I'm going to do today," I said—and I did it. Day two was walking out to the car. Day three, the end of the driveway…you get the idea. By about day six I was two houses down on the sidewalk, where there was a bench where I could rest. And rest, I surely needed. Those walks were incredibly difficult: I'd sweat like a pig in a sausage factory, and the world would just *spiiinnn* as I walked, but each day got a little easier. I'd sweat a little less. The spinning got better. I was making slow, steady progress.

My goal for Halloween was to take Christian, who was coming up on his first birthday, out trick-or-treating. (And by "out" I mean to maybe two or three houses, but still. To me at the time that was OUT out.) Sarah bought him a so-cute-it-made-you-nauseous spaceman costume; we decided we'd make the journey to our next-door neighbors', then if I were up to it, to a house across the street. As it turned out, the home directly across from us had just been bought after being for sale for a while, so we thought it'd be a good chance to introduce ourselves to our new neighbors.

And you'll never believe what happened. We made it over there, and it took a little while with me walking slowly and Sarah's mom Debbie carrying Christian. We rang the doorbell and waited; after a few seconds a woman opened the door. We looked at each other, with me a little cloudy from the painkillers I was still taking…and after a few seconds she said: "Chris *Wiehl*?!"

It took me a second to remember who she was. Then: "Ann *Gilbertson*?" (Ann was a girl I'd known back at U-Dub.)

"Yeah!" she said. "But it's Ann Haggart now. I married Greg!"

"Wait…you…Greg Haggart? My *fraternity brother* Greg Hagg —"

At that point, Greg himself barreled to the door, and parroted his wife. "Chris *Wiehl*???" Turns out they'd moved to L.A. years before—we'd lost touch after college—and Greg was producing commercials. They had two kids, one about Christian's age and one a couple of years older.

And obviously, they didn't know I'd just had brain surgery. "Hey, great costume," Greg said, gesturing to the giant scar on my head. "What are you, some kind of

Frankenstein or something?" He moved in to give me a
bear hug.

"Hey, hey, slow down, big guy," I said as I put out a
hand to stop him. I gave them the story about the tumor
and the surgery, and they couldn't have been more
apologetic and graceful. We said our goodbyes, as I had
to get back home and lie down, then we made the
incredibly long 150-foot journey back across the street.

But how crazy is that? Nearly twenty million people
in the greater L.A. area, and one of my good buddies
from twenty years before—from a whole other *state*—
moved in across the street. Greg and I still laugh about it.
He and I are producing partners now, and he was a
producer on *Worry D—Devil's Dolls*.

So each day, I would progress a *liiittle* more. Having
Debbie there was fantastic; I couldn't do anything to help
care for Christian (and I wouldn't even be able to hold
him for a few weeks yet), so Debbie was a lifesaver. I
would spend each day walking a little bit, trying to relearn how to balance myself, and getting plenty of rest.
And each day I felt a *liiittle* better.

About my hearing: I still wasn't sure whether I could
hear anything in my right ear. At one point, I remember,

I tested it by putting the phone up to my ear—and I could've sworn I heard something. (Not a lot, but anything was better than nothing.) I was excited at the possibility that hey, maybe I could still hear in that ear after all.

Then I learned the real truth.

Sometime after Halloween, Sarah drove me down to House Clinic for a follow-up visit so they could test my hearing. So we got there, and I went into this booth where I put on some headphones, and they played a series of beeps, and they asked me to raise my hand when I heard anything. After the test, I asked the woman who'd performed it about the results. "So? How bout it? Did I…?" And I don't know if she was just having a bad day, or maybe she didn't realize the gravity of what she was saying; in any case, her answer was as cold and flat as a week-old pancake.

"Oh, you're deaf," she said. "You didn't hear a thing." And that was it. Very matter-of-fact.

I just sat there stunned. I got up after a minute and walked back to the room where Sarah was waiting for me.

"Well?" she asked. "How'd it go?"

"I'm…I'm deaf." Those words tasted awful, but they were the truth. Okay, I wasn't *totally* deaf, since my left ear still had a hundred percent of its function, but learning that I'd lost all hearing in the other one was tough. It emphasized the enormity of the rehabilitation that lay ahead; it knocked me off of the "Hey! I'm alive!" pink cloud I'd been riding, and made me feel pretty small. And I realized I'd never be the same man.

I asked my surgeon if he could explain exactly *why* I'd lost my hearing. "As we were coming out [with the surgical tools, I assume he meant], the auditory nerve spasmed." When I asked him why that happened, he said he didn't know; brain and nerve functions are so complex, he said, that he had no scientific explanation for it. Whether the nerve spasm happened naturally or due to human error, I'll never know. I *do* know that the surgeons did the best they could, and unfortunately I came out on the forty-percent side of losing my hearing. I took a chance—and it's a chance I'd take again.

So life—my *new* life—continued. I put all my focus on daily goals, and little by little, I started feeling more like my former self. (Though I knew I would never totally *be* my old self, I wanted to work to get as close as possible to being pre-tumor Chris.) And taking things one step at a time really helped me avoid any serious depression. I remember several of my friends and/or colleagues coming by the house for lunch in those early weeks post-surgery: my manager Mark and my agent Dan "On to the Next" Baron, among others. They helped me focus on my future instead of getting bogged down in my past. My buddy Ted Ackerley (who's also from Washington, and was an executive producer on *Wor — Devil's Dolls*) actually said, "You need to get healthy enough so we can go climb Mount Rainier." And though we haven't done the climb yet, we plan to; that support and encouragement, from Ted and many other people, was an unbelievable help in keeping my spirits up during those dark days.

My folks came down for Thanksgiving, and it was great to see them again. (If memory serves, Debbie had gone home by that point.) And Thanksgiving morning was the annual Turkey Trot charity race I talked about before. "Holy shit, Chris, you didn't run *that* year, did you?!" you might be asking.

And the answer is: yes. Well, sort of.

The race always starts with a timed mile. And I decided I would give the mile a shot and see if I could make it. I'd run the race before, and I think I'd done the mile in about five and a half minutes the previous year (not great, but not shabby either, especially for a guy in his late thirties). Mom and Dad ran it too, but there was a lot of focus on me trying to run a mile only a month after brain surgery.

I ran the entire mile. Coach English would've been proud, because that bear was on my back before I even friggin' *started*. My balance was still pretty bad—mainly, it was my "vertical hold" that was still out of tune—and I overextended myself. I must've looked pretty silly, because I was all over the track toward the end. But you know what? *I did it*. My time was a little over eight minutes.

Everybody in attendance—including me—was thrilled. One guy there named Johnnie Morton, a retired NFL receiver, cried; he said it was one of the bravest things he'd ever seen. In retrospect, it was probably more stupid than brave, but it was something I needed to do. Running, as you know, has always been a huge part of my life, so to run that mile—even if I looked ridiculous doing it—was incredibly affirming. And I consider that Turkey Trot as the unofficial beginning of my comeback. It was the first scene in The Return of Christopher Wiehl.

* * * *

By the time we rang in the New Year of 2010, I was definitely on the comeback trail. I'd started jogging again, and my balance issues had improved some, though I continued to wobble a bit when I walked, and I was pretty clumsy. I also got dizzy in dark places where I couldn't really focus on inanimate objects—movie theaters and similar places were not fun. And I would turn to my left to investigate sounds from my right side. (Shoot, even seven years later I still have trouble discerning the directions of sounds, and I figure I always will—but I'm learning to compensate by looking left *and* right when I hear something not in my direct field of vision.)

That Christmas had been okay. We'd flown back East to visit Sarah's parents, and it was pretty tough for me. All that *movement*! Walking through the airports, flying in a plane…hell, just walking around was still pretty taxing. And probably the most difficult thing to come to terms with was the fact that I was now hearing-impaired; it was probably tougher mentally and emotionally than it was physically. What did being partially deaf mean for my career? When would I be able to come back to acting? (For the record, my doctors said I wouldn't be able to work for at least a year; it was one of my top priorities to prove them wrong. And as you'll see, I was able to do just that.) What kept me going at that point—what kept me *sane*—was focusing on those daily goals. As each day passed, I'd improve the tiniest bit. It was the whole "step over each pebble, and eventually you'll cross the entire mountain" thing. And little by little, it worked.

That February, an old friend named Danny Kolker came back to town after living in Louisville for a while, and he moved into our guest house. At that point, I wasn't back on the acting horse yet, so I got busy writing. Danny told me about the germ of an idea he had about some dolls that make people go nuts, so we commenced to working on a screenplay that eventually became *Worry Dolls*. (Which itself eventually became *The Devil's Dolls*. Dammit.)

Within the next month, the acting itch became too strong not to scratch, so I started going on auditions again when pilot season cranked up. And it was too soon. Casting directors would call my manager Mark to express their concern that something wasn't right with me (and a couple of them even thought I'd been drinking before the audition). And that put Mark in a difficult space. We'd decided that we didn't want the tumor/surgery business to go public, because the Hollywood grapevine is just vicious. Word gets out that you have (or even *had*) a medical issue, then you're marked as damaged goods, and you're essentially done for…so Mark had to just kind of play it off and be noncommittal about it. There were a few offers I had to pass on because the physical demands were too great. And I think Mark actually did tell a few people he trusted, so word about my surgery (and my rehabilitation from it) got out a little bit, but the overall damage to my professional reputation was minimal. Thank *God*.

But then, at the end of March, I was blessed to be offered a job without even having to audition for it. In 2008 I'd had a supporting role in a Hallmark Christmas movie called *Moonlight & Mistletoe*, so the Hallmark people were familiar with my work. Lo and behold, they called and asked if I wanted the lead opposite Christine Taylor (Ben Stiller's wife, about whom I'd heard good things) in *Farewell Mr. Kringle*, another holiday movie that was set to begin filming in April. Mark and I discussed it, and I decided to give it a go. I'd read the script, and realized there weren't a lot of physical demands (I mean, c'mon, it was a Christmas movie. It was just people walking around speaking sappy dialogue). Mark and I figured the Hallmark people didn't know about my medical issue, because they offered me the role no questions asked. So we decided we'd keep that under wraps for the time being and see how it went.

We started the shoot out in Simi Valley (and I realized that on one of those first days it was April 13—exactly six months after my surgery), and it was exhausting. I remember having to go lie down in my trailer between takes; my energy level was extremely low compared to my pre-surgery days. After a week or two, I ended up telling my co-star Christine and the director that I'd recently had brain surgery, just in case they were wondering about my lack of stamina and/or my difficulty in hearing things, and they couldn't have been more gracious and understanding. So we got through it. And that role, at that time, was indeed a blessing: for one thing, it gave me some much-needed confidence that I could still perform, but it also made me realize that my doctors had been right. I *wasn't* ready, especially for roles that required a lot of physical exertion. (I mean, shoot—I'd only recently been cleared to *sneeze*, for cryin' out loud!) I knew I'd eventually get back in physical shape, but it would be a while yet.

But doing that movie put me back on the performing horse. I really had to ease my way back into it, but heck, I was just glad I was back in it at all! Within the next year or so, I guest-starred on an episode of the ABC crime drama *Body of Proof*, then I had a recurring role on ABC Family's *Switched at Birth*. Doing *Switched* was cool; I originally read for one of the leads in the pilot and thought I had a good shot at getting it. But then they cast Lea Thompson as the wife of the character I'd read for, and I was just too young to play Lea's husband. (They ended up giving it to a guy named D.W. Moffett, who's great, so no big whoop.) But not long after the show got picked up by ABC Family, they called and asked if I wanted to play Patrick, the love interest to one of the series leads. I was in seven episodes. And the cool thing was that deafness was a big part of the show. One of the lead characters—Daphne, one of the two girls "switched at birth"—was deaf. (Katie LeClerc, the actress who played her, wasn't completely deaf herself, but she *was* hearing-impaired.) So hearing impairment was a big theme; Daphne's best friend Emmett (played by deaf actor Sean Berdy) and Emmett's mother (the incredible Marlee Matlin) are both deaf, so there were scenes shot entirely in American Sign Language. To my knowledge, the show was the first mainstream TV series to have deafness at the forefront of its storyline. All that to say that being on that show gave me a real sense of comfort about my own hearing loss. It made me stop and realize that my hearing impairment wasn't such a terrible thing—it just was what it was.

Speaking of hearing impairment: doing those episodes of *Switched at Birth* made me realize that I'd had to change my acting technique somewhat. For one thing, since I was now half-deaf, I had to really focus and concentrate on, and *listen* to, the other characters in a scene so I could make sure I heard their lines. And if you know anything about acting, you'll realize this was also a good thing. I'd done it to an extent before the tumor, but now listening intensely was a necessity; if anything, it probably sharpened my acting skills.

I also had to learn to pace myself, and conserve energy whenever possible. Reason being: at the end of a day, by 5:00 or 6:00, I would just be *exhausted*. It was partly because I hadn't redeveloped my endurance after the surgery, but I also realized there was another factor playing in: I had to strain more to listen, and doing so created a lot of body tension. And the logic follows that if you tense muscles nonstop for a long time (which I was now doing when I strained to hear other actors), the muscles will fatigue more quickly. I had to sort of train myself to relax my body whenever I could. In the years since, I've gotten better at it, partly because I've become more used to hearing things with only my left ear, but even now, I *still* get worn out at the end of a long day of filming.

So as the months went by, I became more acquainted with my "new normal," and thus more comfortable with it. Unfortunately, though, life on the home front was anything *but* normal. It was marvelous watching Christian grow from an infant, to a toddler, then to a little boy…but at that point, Sarah and I were growing even further apart. It's like we were speaking two completely different languages. The therapy sessions that we'd been attending for forever, it seemed like, didn't seem to be helping. At one point I remember Sarah saying something like: "Well, there are times in every marriage where you're just going to hate each other. That's just the way it is, and we need to find a way to work through it." And I remember thinking, "Uh, no. I don't agree with that. At *all*." We just weren't walking through life together anymore.

I remember that we went to Hilton Head again (Sarah's parents had a great place on the island) in the spring of 2012, and at that point she and I were barely speaking. When we got back, things between us sort of came to a head. In our next therapy session, our analyst confirmed my belief that our marriage wasn't headed in the right direction. At one point, I remember, I asked him what would be best for little Christian (who was three then), and his response was both heartbreaking and perfectly logical.

"Well, if you get a divorce now," he said, "Christian will never remember you together."

Within a month, I'd moved out.

Chapter 13:
Ten Minutes, Ten Months, Ten Years

(Dec. 13)

It's mid-December now, and at the Wiehl house the proverbial sleigh bells are ringing. Our tree is up already, and we got three nice, deep new stockings for the kids to collect plenty of Santa's bounty.

Like most folks, I love Christmastime. Being with family, the festive spirit, just the sense of togetherness, I think, is beautiful. It's an attitude of joy, isn't it? Growing up, the holiday season was unique in our household. My mom is Danish, remember, and one tradition for Danes is to put real candles on their Christmas trees. (If you've ever seen a tree lit with real candles, you know how spectacular it is.) But doing this required a pretty good-sized tree, with branches strong enough to hold the candles' weight. So every year we'd get a permit to go cut our own tree up in the Cascade Mountains (God's church, remember?). And of course, Mom never wanted a tree right by the road; we'd hike through snow into some dense underbrush, and there, right at the edge of a dangerous cliff, would be Mom's

226

choice of the perfect tree. We'd bring it home, put thirty or so candles on it (along with more traditional decorations, too), then we'd have these parties where Dad would light the candles, and we'd all stand around the tree and sing Christmas hymns. It was an unbelievably special time; I have really fond memories of those singalongs next to our gorgeous candlelit tree.

But this year, Christmas at our house will be a more intimate, cozy affair. We had some of the extended family—my parents and Sharon's mom—with us for Thanksgiving, so for Christmas it's just going to be our immediate family: me, Sharon, Christian, Brett, and Trista. Us and the three monkeys. It's the beginning, I hope, of a new tradition of "familyhood" for all of us. We're in our new house, and it's the first Christmas for Sharon and me as a married couple, so it's sort of a new beginning for us. Watching the kids opening their gifts on Christmas morning, having an intimate family Christmas dinner—it'll all be meaningful.

As I write this section, too, I'm thinking about how interesting it is that the meaning of Christmas changes as we age. Know what I mean? When I was a kid, Christmastime, of course, meant getting stuff: I'd get plenty of gifts, obviously, and I'd also get time off from school. But as I got older, the "stuff I got" was different: in my twenties and thirties, I'd get to go home and see my parents, and I'd get a lot of much-needed rest. And now that I'm on the cusp of middle age, I get the joy that comes from giving to others. Watching my kids' eyes light up when they open gifts? There isn't anything much better in this life. And I think about how I was that kid once. That was forty years ago, but it seems like the blink of an eye.

Life can be *so* damn quick. And I think it's important to have a good foundation for it. *That's* what I'm trying to get at here. Having a beautiful, safe atmosphere to come to every day—having a *home*—is incredibly important.

And it wasn't so long ago that I wondered whether I'd ever have a home again at all.

* * * *

The official Webster's definition of "therapy" is: "treatment intended to relieve or heal a disorder." Unfortunately for Sarah and me, even after years of therapy to try and save our marriage, there was very little relief or healing going on. So when our therapist posited the idea that divorce, while Christian was still young, might be better, I figured that was the least painful course of action.

There's no doubt that leaving my wife was the most difficult, heartbreaking decision I've ever had to make. It's a pretty well-known fact that, next to the death of a loved one, divorce is the most stressful situation human beings endure. The person who'd been your best friend, your confidant, your *partner* in life, becomes your adversary. That said, I feel like the decision I made was the best one (or the least hurtful one, I guess) for Sarah and Christian, as well as for me—*especially* in the long term. I felt at that point that if anything, our relationship was only going to get worse, so it was better to end it then and avert any further difficulties for the three of us.

Within a couple of days of that revelatory therapy session, I sat Sarah down and told her that our marriage was over, and I was leaving. First I stayed with my friends Phil and Kathy for a few weeks, then I found a tiny studio apartment in Santa Monica, and set about the horrible-but-necessary task of moving some essential items out of the house and into my new place.

Once I got settled in…there I was. I was on my own, a single man, for the first time in ten years. I'd just been through a tough ordeal physically with the brain tumor, and then to deal with this sudden emotional trauma was almost too much. I was just numb for a while (and I'll admit I self-medicated some to bolster that numbness), but I also had plenty of time to contemplate the decision I'd made, and think about life in general. And as time went by, I continued to believe I'd made the right choice in leaving. As me being the leav*er* and not the leav*ee,* if that makes sense, I knew I'd have to shoulder a lot of the blame, and that's understandable. But I believed (and in retrospect, I'm now *convinced*) that it was the right thing to do. We were just too different. We tried to make it work. It didn't. When it came down to it, a divorce was going to be less painful than continuing our marriage. Sad as it was, that was how I felt. It's how I still feel now. And if Christian ever asks why we divorced, I'll tell him what I just told you. In painfully simple terms, I'll tell him, it was best for Mommy and Daddy to live separately. That's about the size of it.

I will say, too, that I'm just as much at fault as Sarah is. I wholeheartedly acknowledge that being married to me must not have been easy for her in some respects. As a professional actor, there's a lot of uncertainty about my job (and therefore about me): I have to travel a lot, sometimes with very little advance notice; and since I don't have a typical forty-hour workweek, my schedule and my financial standing are often difficult to predict. Since Sarah wasn't familiar with the entertainment industry when we started our relationship, dealing with that sort of unpredictability must've been difficult. Listen: as mother to my son, I'll always love Sarah, and I'll always be thankful that she brought Christian into the world. I'll also dearly miss the daily interaction with my in-laws. I know that my leaving caused all of them a lot of pain, and for that, I will always be truly sorry.

For a few months, that was how things stood: me in an apartment, and her in the house, as we both started to put our lives back together. Then in the fall of 2012, they moved to a condo a few blocks away, and I moved back into the house. We started some divorce mediation, but...let me say that on top of everything else, Sarah had also developed some health issues at that point. She'd suffered from various ailments for a few years, but in 2012 she was diagnosed with Lyme disease. She went to numerous doctors for treatment, few of whom seemed able to help her much. So, unfortunately, in addition to our separation, she had her health to worry about.

Nevertheless, the divorce proceedings moved forward. It was incredibly humbling, embarrassing, and painful—all those negative words attached to a divorce are absolutely true. Even so, we had to get through it. And we did. The divorce was finalized by the end of the year—it was actually pretty quick. We didn't fight much, which was good, but the process was still pretty dismal. We went through some mediation and met with several counselors to resolve our issues. I tried to be as fair as I could, especially when it came to dividing up our possessions. I feel that in a lot of ways, I settled on some things that I didn't really want to settle on—but the kicker is, I'm sure Sarah felt the same way. That's just the nature of divorce. No one is to blame—but at the same time, *both* are to blame. It's incredibly difficult for everybody involved. In the end, we both wanted to act in the best interests of our son, and I think we did that.

Before we move on, I want to tell you about one situation in all that horror that has stuck with me. It was something a family law attorney talked about at one of our mediations: the Ten-Ten-Ten Rule. If somebody (namely, your soon-to-be former spouse) does something to piss you off—I mean, something that *really* makes your blood boil—think about how you'll feel about it in ten minutes. Odds are, you'll still be angry; at that point, consider whether you'll still be mad in ten months. Then repeat the process, and consider how you'll feel (and if you'll even remember!) in ten *years*. It's a nearly foolproof way to curtail a lot of anger and hurt feelings.

And there was one instance during those painful divorce proceedings in which I used the Ten-Ten-Ten Rule to great advantage. One of the suggestions in our mediation was for us to each go through our house and put colored stickers on the items (furniture, decorations, etcetera) we wanted. So we did that; Sarah went first, and when it was my turn, I went through and marked my own. Sarah had put stickers on a lot of items that I wanted too, but I acquiesced. But then, there were two great paintings in the living room, and I thought it was fair that I get at least one of them. Sarah, however, had marked them both. I'll spare you the details, other than that I completely flipped. In the midst of my tirade, though, I remembered: Ten-Ten-Ten. I stopped yelling and went for a walk, and that did the trick. During that walk—which took about ten minutes, of course—I asked myself how I'd feel about those paintings in ten months, and then in ten years. *If I'm still pissed about whether or not I have certain "stuff" in ten years, I need to get a life*, I joked inwardly.

I got back to the house and told Sarah she could have both of them. And now, when I go to Sarah's house to get Christian, and I see those paintings on the wall? I'm like, *Eh. I'm glad she's enjoying them.* Because life's too short, man. There's too much stuff to worry about to let yourself get all bent out of shape over little things. Ten-Ten-Ten.

* * * *

From 2012 until 2014 or so is a period of my life I consider as my unofficial rebirth. And it was a sort of restoration on several fronts: I was still recovering physically from the brain surgery, and after Sarah and I parted ways I had to recover emotionally and spiritually as well. Life as a newly single man was difficult at first; I was scared, unsure, and anxious, and creatively, I was about as productive as a toilet brush. It was just…for a while I had no idea of the direction my life would take.

But little by little, I began turning things around. As is typical for divorcees, I threw myself into work. Danny Kolker and I had finished the first draft of *Worry Dolls*, so I made it my life's mission to get the damn thing produced. (And with the help of my cherished friend Ted Ackerley, things were set in motion.) As you probably know, making an independent film is an absolutely *monstrous* task. We had to do script rewrites, yes, but we also had to find a director, a good cast and crew, and we had to figure out how to raise about a million dollars. That was the tough part. Little by little, I found investors who donated $25,000 here, $50,000 there, and a lot of those investors were back home in Washington, so I spent a ton of time on planes traveling between L.A. and Seattle. It took a while to raise the money, but I finally got it done.

We found a great director for it too: a guy named Padraig Reynolds, a horror writer/director known for the film *Rites of Spring*, among other things. He seemed to share a similar vision for the film as Danny and I did; he also said the script needed to be cut down to a more workable size, so we did yet *another* rewrite. But once that was done…we had the green light. Finally— *finally!*—we went to Mississippi in the fall of 2014 to shoot the film. Why Mississippi? A couple of reasons: one, it was cheaper, and two, we believed the atmosphere of the Deep South gave the film the best feel. We spent about seven weeks shooting in the Jackson area, Canton, Vicksburg, and Natchez, and we came home extremely pleased with the results.

Unfortunately, upon my return, the ugliness of divorce reared its head once more. Sarah, as I said, had learned a couple years before that she was suffering from Lyme disease, and she eventually expressed to me her desire to move to a place where she could get better treatment for it. She originally wanted to move somewhere back East, but there was no way I would agree to that, as my son would just be too far away; we finally compromised, and she found a place in Santa Rosa, a few miles north of San Francisco and closer to specialists in the Bay Area. By the first week of November, she and Christian were gone.

Her moving up there has been something I've struggled with ever since. One the one hand, I truly want Sarah to have the best health she can…but on the other, I miss my boy. I went from seeing Christian every day to seeing him one weekend a month, holidays, and summers. I'd coached his baseball and soccer teams when he was here. I was an *everyday influence on his life*, and after he moved away, I was no longer that. It's been a source of pain ever since. But the way I see it, raising a child is a marathon undertaking, and in the long run, Sarah's health is the most important factor. Even so, it's still horribly painful not having my son as part of my everyday world. How do I deal with it? I keep walking forward, of course.

* * * *

There are a couple other factors that played into this Rebirth period for me. One is that I got a new acting coach. His name is James Reese, and he's taken my approach to acting further than I ever imagined it could go.

Once Sarah's and my divorce process started, I felt like a ship at sea, I guess. So to try and stay focused, I buried myself in work. In addition to producing *Worry Dolls*, I wanted to move forward with my acting, and it was a case of total serendipity that I ran into James one day at a commercial audition. I'd worked with him years before, and he was now working with the agency that was casting the commercial for which I was auditioning. At one point, he and I were talking out in the hall, and I was admiring some great photos that were on the wall. When he told me that he was the one who shot those photos, one thing led to another, and he agreed to shoot some new headshots for me. That day I discovered that James is an excellent photographer—he shot the photo on the cover of this book, matter of fact—and not only that, he coaches actors too. "Well," I asked him, "how about we work together on my next audition?" And he's been my coach ever since. He's helped me rediscover my passion for acting.

God's honest truth: James is incredible. He works my ass off, and as a good coach should (whether in

acting, sports, or anything else), he gets me to reach my
peak performance level. He helps me discover a
character's layers, a character's life outside scenes,
and—more than any other coach/mentor I've ever had—
he helps me *deconstruct the language* of the words my
characters speak. That's huge. For every audition I go on
or role I play, we'll spend time breaking the words apart;
he'll offer suggestions on various ways to speak each
phrase, even going so far as working with my voice
register. "Maybe try going down on this sentence," he'll
say. Or, "Try whispering this next line." Oftentimes I
will have only a single day to work on a character before
an audition, and James helps me find the little details
within the scene. And *that's* what the producers and
directors remember. "Oh, that's interesting. We haven't
seen that," you hope they say after your audition—and
it's one more step toward booking the gig. In essence,
James has helped me find the *gravitas* in my acting. That
sense of gravity was always within me; I just never knew
how to find it until I started working with him. James has
helped me find the extra step in the acting race.

    With James's help, I landed a guest-starring role on
the ABC drama *Revenge*, and my episode aired in March

of 2015. Then—*then*—I got a role in what's been one of my favorite guest-starring appearances to date: Showtime's *Masters of Sex*, a drama chronicling the lives of acclaimed sexual research scientists Masters and Johnson during the 1950s and -60s. In the episode, which aired in August of '15, I played Al Neely, a retired NFL star who was married to a famous Hollywood starlet. (The couple, I think, was sort of modeled after Joe DiMaggio and Marilyn Monroe's brief, torrid relationship.) We go to Masters and Johnson to get them to help us save our marriage; they couldn't, mainly because my character was screwing everybody in town, but our meeting helped them raise awareness of their research to near-celebrity level. (And to answer your question: *No*, I didn't get naked in the episode. What's that? Oh, you didn't ask? Oh well. In any case, no nudity for me.) James and I worked hard on that one, and it was a ton of fun to shoot. And doing that episode reminded me that hey, I was pretty good at this acting thing.

Working with James, getting *Worry Dolls* pro—oh sorry. Getting *DEVIL'S Dolls* produced, doing more acting in general—they were part of that rebirth I've talked about. I was breathing new life into my career.

Personally though, I was still sort of adrift, and I was a little lonely, especially after Christian moved away with his mom. So what do people in search of companionship do in these days of modern technology?

Right. They download dating apps.

I joined Tinder in late 2014, and I started the ol' "swipe left, swipe right" business…and one of the first women I swiped right on (meaning I liked her) was a gorgeous blonde named Sharon. She likewise swiped right, we set up a first date, and it went extremely well. We're both Scorpios, and we're both high-energy, positive people; we just had an incredible amount of stuff in common. Plus, I learned on that first date that Sharon was a divorced mom with two kids about Christian's age. The commonalities were unbelievable!

We fell for each other. Fell *hard*. Right away, we realized we had an immensely positive effect on one another. We lifted each other up. We made each other *shine*. And that's the sort of relationship I'd been looking for my entire adult life. I had absolutely no plans to ever get married again—but as Sharon and I grew closer, marrying her seemed like the most natural thing in the world. We got engaged on Christmas Eve, 2015, and as you know, we married in July.

We both like to say that we met each other exactly when we were both ready, and not a moment before or after. Our relationship is fantastic, but it took us both going through a lot of adversity for that to be the case: both our divorces, my brain tumor, Sharon's dad passing away too soon…all those roads led us to each other. And it's beautiful.

We've both been through a good bit of therapy, and I think we're using what we've learned in those sessions to great advantage. Sharon, for her part, doesn't put up with my crap. She sets clear boundaries; long as I don't cross them, things are great, but if I *do* cross the line, she won't hesitate to call me on it. (And it's beautiful how reminiscent that is of my parents and their three-point-oh-oh-oh GPA rule.) The best thing about our union is that it's rooted in love, respect, communication, and empathy. There's very little manipulation or condescension going on. We're a happy and healthy couple. With her kids Brett and Trista, and my son Christian, we're a blended family. We're a *happy* family. And once again, it's beautiful.

* * * *

So…yeah. I think that pretty much brings us to the present, doesn't it?

Our walk's almost over.

Chapter 14:
Arrival

We're almost there.

Pretty soon, we'll arrive at our destination. Can you see it? Or maybe the more appropriate question is: Can you *feel* it?

We're almost there. And when I say that, you might interpret "there" in a couple of different ways: you may construe it as the "destination" of the allegorical walk we've taken within these pages. Or shoot, you might simply interpret it literally as the end of this book.

It's both. The destination is called…well, before I get into that, and before this book actually comes to an end, I want to mention a couple of things. Some "acts of culmination," if you will, here at the finish. That cool with you?

Okay, first: throughout these pages, I've talked about a sort of "agreement" I made with a high school friend about how we hoped to do something important with our lives, and how we revisited that at our reunions. She always said I "won" because of my celebrity status; I disagreed by saying that her stability trumped my fame. Remember all that?

Well, the tides have turned. As you know, I'm now married again—and *happily* so—and I recently found out that my friend got a divorce after about twenty years of what I'd thought was a happy marriage. I'm not being judgmental or exploitative; I know from experience that divorce sucks, and I feel horrible that my friend has had to endure marital strife too.

So that brings up a question: who is more successful? And I think the answer is both of us, and neither of us. At the risk of sounding cliché here, success is what you make of it. It may be that my friend is happier now that she's single, and they were miserable for years before they split up. For me, though my career is not cooking as much as it has before, I feel as successful as I've ever felt being part of a happy, *stable* family. My point is this: Life is valuable. Things change. So count your lucky stars whenever you possibly can— even if they're hard to see.

I've also realized as John and I have been putting these chapters together, that there's a whole array of little tidbits about my career as a working actor that might be helpful to people just starting out. A lot of these are things I've learned through experience that would've been great to know from the beginning, and would've saved me a lot of heartache, so I'd like to pass on what I've learned. Listen: by *no means* do I think I know it all. Simple talent—and simple *luck*—play as much of a part in an actor's success as does anything else. But this is a list of things that, when combined with some talent and good luck, might help create some opportunity. And I'll be repeating some things from earlier, but I think it'll be useful to tie it all together here, so bear with me. I also realize that these might be clichés, but they're clichés for a reason: unless you ascribe to them, you simply won't make it. The entertainment business is brutal, and nobody's going to hand you a break. *Nobody.* With that in mind:

--Do something to help your career, and your craft, *every single day.* And by "every day," I mean seven days a week, 365 days a year. Audition. Read a play. Exercise. Talk to other actors. Go *see* a play, or a movie. Read acting trade magazines. Take a class. Sing. Practice monologues. Practice. Practice. Practice. Being a professional actor is an enormous commitment—much more so, I think, than almost any other profession. It's your *life*, pretty much. So to get that "extra step," you gotta work harder than the next guy. And hear me when I say this: if you're not willing to commit *everything* to it, find another line of work. I mean that.

--Stay sharp—both mentally *and* physically. Every good carpenter takes great care of his tools; he keeps them in a special box, and he cleans and maintains them regularly. Why? Because they're his means of livelihood. As an actor, your tool, your means of livelihood, is your body — both your physical makeup and your mind. So try to keep both in good shape. For one, exercise often, because you want to be able to handle any physical challenge a role might present (and *believe me*, there will be some). And two: *read*. Every day. Whether it's books, plays, scripts, or whatever, reading and interpreting words keeps you mentally acquainted with language—and obviously, language is a fundamental part of acting. So constant reading, I think, is a mental version of jogging.

--Have an open mind, but also wear blinders. In other words, stay focused. Being open to new ideas, new changes, etcetera, is great, but there are a lot of times when you have to shut things out. I'll explain: early in my career, I would drive through Hollywood and see all these stars on billboards, or I'd see the latest feature about "The Hot New Hollywood Actor!" on *Entertainment Tonight*, and I'd get frustrated. "Dammit, why not *me*???" would run through my head. And I had to learn to ignore that and stay focused on bettering myself. I did so by concentrating on doing the first two things in this list: staying sharp, and performing daily tasks to advance my career. And I'll advise others just starting out to do the same. Because, you know, reality. If you stay mentally and physically sharp, and do something every day to better yourself, you'll be ready when (or more accurately, *if*) you get an opportunity. If you don't, then you have no chance at all.

And that brings me to the last item. And this is a big one.

--Learn to live with disappointment. An actor I know named Kevin O'Rourke, who has worked regularly in TV and film for nearly forty years, once broke it down for me. I was right out of college, and what he told me has stuck with me ever since. He said: "If you book one out of every thirty auditions, you'll be a success." Think about that. You put everything you have into these auditions, hopefully, and twenty-nine out of thirty times, you're told you're not good enough. And even then, even if the one job of thirty you book has tons of promise and is going to make you The Hot New Hollywood Actor…odds are, that won't end up happening. (Remember *Bronx County*? Or *Bull*? Or even *Playmakers*? I thought all three of those shows were my ticket, and none of them were.) The entertainment industry is fickle and unpredictable, and nothing is guaranteed—least of all, actors' job security. If you can handle that, if you can keep that constant disappointment from taking over your life, you have a shot. And *that's* the X-factor. *That's* what separates the great ones. The longer you can keep trying, the…less long the odds become, if that makes sense.

So there you have it. To those of you just getting started, I say: I wish you the best. But I'll also say that your odds of being successful are pretty slim. I hope you're okay with that. If you are, give 'em hell. And maybe I'll see you at an audition sometime.

* * * *

One thing I've realized as I've worked on this book is: I have a beautiful life. It hasn't always been that way, and I've made a *ton* of mistakes during my forty-six years on this planet, but I've tried (with moderate success) to learn from those mistakes so I don't repeat them. Something else I've been doing lately—mainly at my wife Sharon's insistence—is celebrating the small victories. Example: earlier in my career, when I'd book a guest-starring role on a show, I wouldn't be content with it. I'd constantly be scheming: will this role turn into a recurring one? How can I parlay this into more work in the future? I was always thinking of the next thing—so much so that I couldn't enjoy the present. I was constantly "on to the next," without allowing myself to realize that the place I was currently in was pretty damn sweet.

That has changed for me. When I recently booked that episode of *NCIS*, Sharon made a special dinner, and we celebrated. And during the episode shoot, I just enjoyed being there, enjoyed the whole filming process—I enjoyed the moments. And *that's* a big part of why my life is beautiful now: because I'm *learning to live in the moment.* I'm learning to appreciate the things I have, instead of worrying about the things I don't. And that, my friend, is the key. When I can do that, instead of "*trying* to walk *like* a man," I can walk *as* a man. I can love who I am; I can love *what* I am.

And what am I? I'm a man. I'm thinking now of a great Teddy Roosevelt quote, one of my all-time favorites; I don't remember it word-for-word, so I'll paraphrase. But it really speaks to who I am:

"It's not the critic who counts. It's not the man who points out how the strong man stumbles. The credit belongs to the man who is actually in the arena, whose face is covered by sweat, dust and blood; who fails again and again, but still strives to do great deeds. But his place shall never be with the timid souls who know neither victory nor defeat."

One of my personal creeds is: To live an exceptional life, you have to put in the work. I've worked extremely hard to create the life I have now. It's been unbelievably tough sometimes. I've had a lot of pain, and a lot of joy.

And all of it—the disappointments, the victories, the uncertainties, the changes, the sadness, the satisfaction, the love, the *life*—have brought me to where I am at this moment. I've arrived here a man. And we're both here. We're *here*.

Look around. You like it? This is a place I come to as often as I can. Unfortunately, I never stay. But I keep coming back here whenever possible. What's its name? I'm pretty sure we call it the same thing.

Happiness.

As is life, we can't stay here forever; if we did, we probably wouldn't be living a true life, would we? But look around. What does yours look like?

I'll tell you what mine is. It's a lot of different things; not "places," necessarily, but states of being. It's when I hug my son, and look into his face and see a reflection of my own. It's laughing with Sharon. It's picking up Brett or Trista when they cry. It's discovering new meaning in the text of a script when I'm working with James. It's sweating like a dog when I do the

Saturday exercise class at Burn Fitness. It's learning something new from my parents. It's being…alive.

I'm alive. And so are you. There was a time when I thought I might not live much longer, but I did. I made it through. And so have you. And for the time we have left here, let's walk as men or women.

Thanks for walking with me. I hope you've enjoyed the journey as much as I have.

See you back here soon.

Acknowledgments

Christopher Wiehl thanks:

Writing a book has always been a goal of mine; without the extreme talent and insight of John Turner, this could not have been possible.

To people who have supported me during my career: my manager Mark Armstrong and everyone at Sanders/Armstrong/Caserta Management; my agent Dan Baron and everyone at Agency for the Performing Arts; and all the fine agents at AKA Talent Agency.

To the *Worry Dolls* producing team: Ted Ackerley, Greg Haggart, and Greg Root.

And of course, thank you to the never-ending support of my family: my parents, Lis, and Brett and Trista.

To my loving, supporting wife, Sharon.

And finally, to my son Christian, who inspires me to walk like a man.

John Turner thanks:

My beautiful wife Kari for her continued love, support, and encouragement, and for her on-the-spot editorial advice. You've made me—and this book—infinitely better. I love you, sweetness.

My dearly departed mother, for instilling in me a love for words, for people, and for how people interpret words. I miss you, Mom.

My new friend, the inimitable Chris Wiehl. It's your openness, courage, and strength that have made this project what it is. On to the next!!!

Author Bios

Christopher Wiehl is an American born actor and filmmaker. Born and raised in Yakima Washington, Chris Graduated from the University of Washington in 1993 with a major in Dramatic Arts. Excited to get into film and television he migrated to Los Angeles in the summer of 94. Chris hit the ground running booking several major Advertising campaigns for Old Spice, Coors, Ford, and Coca-Cola to name a few. In addition to commercial and print campaigns he also appeared as a Guest Star on countless popular television series. This quickly lead him into being series regular world by 1997. i.e.: Bull, First Monday, Playmakers, CSI Las Vegas, Love Monkey and Jericho.

In 1998, Yakima Productions was born. Adding writer, producer, director to his already extensive Bio. Yakima Productions has released 3 films and currently houses over 15 scripts.

Chris' life took a real turn in 2009 when he received a brain tumor diagnosis. With his baby boy only a month old and a marriage already on the rocks, Christopher's life was in peril. He was given a choice to begin radiation or attempt brain surgery for immediate removal of the tumor. Chris had a successful surgery however had major complications through his recovery. It's been a long climb back to relevance in the entertainment world and redemption in his personal world.

Christopher battled back in the years following his brain surgery and today is healthy and happy again, working in Hollywood and living at the beach. A life he thought was out of reach just a few years before.

John Turner is a native Mississippian currently residing in Los Angeles. A 1997 graduate of the University of Southern Mississippi (BFA, Acting/Music), John relocated to New York in 1999 to begin his acting career; in 2002, he was the victim of a brutal mugging and assault, and suffered a traumatic brain injury in the attack. After that incident, John no longer had the physical capabilities to perform, so he established a career as a writer. John recollects the terrible mugging (along with other life lessons) in his first novel, a collection of humorous short stories called "Confessions of a Gimp."

In 2014 John relocated to California to be with the love of his life, his wife Kari.